T0126540

INCULTURATION

Working Papers on Living Faith and Cultures

edited by

Arij A. Roest Crollius, S.J.

XVII

CENTRE "CULTURES AND RELIGIONS" - PONTIFICAL GREGORIAN UNIVERSITY

THE FASCINATING GOD

A Challenge to Modern Chinese Theology
Presented by a Text on the Name of God
Written by a 17th Century Chinese Student of Theology

by

NICOLAS STANDAERT, S.J.

ROME 1995

EDITRICE PONTIFICIA UNIVERSITÀ GREGORIANA
Piazza della Pilotta, 35 - 00187 Roma

世儒非不口口言天，而實則以天爲高遠，耳目不接；若
西士言天，直以爲毛裡之相屬，呼吸喘息之相通，此于
警省人世，最爲親切。

"It is not that the scholars of this world avoid speaking about Heaven,
but they consider Heaven as something too high and distant, so
that the eye or ear cannot perceive it.
But when Westerners speak about Heaven, they consider it as close as
one hair to another, or as the connection of inhaling and
exhaling in breathing, making the human world appreciate that
[Heaven] is most affectionate and intimate."

Excerpt from Chief Grand Secretary Ye Xianggao's 葉向高 (1559-1627)
Preface to the *Xixue shijie chujie* 西學十誡初解 [First Explanation of
the Ten Commandments of Western Learning] (1624).

Table of Contents

Introduction: 17th Century Chinese Students of Theology

The object of this book is the name of the Christian God in Chinese language. We will not, however, attempt to make an exhaustive study. Taking a text of a 17th century Chinese Christian author as our starting point, we will focus only on the names of *Shangdi, Tian* and *Tianzhu* and try to elaborate a fundamental theological reflection on these concepts.

Since the text and the author we use as starting point are relatively unknown, by way of introduction, we would like to indicate the place of 17th century Chinese students of theology in the process of inculturation today.

In a very general way, Catholic theology in this century has undergone some of the following major changes: theologians have rediscovered the Sacred Scriptures; they read Patristic theology with new insight; and they have entered into dialogue with contemporary philosophy, sociology, psychology, and other disciplines. These aspects were not absent in the past, but have come to the surface in a dramatic way during this century resulting in a large amount of creative thinking and of new publication.

Another recent evolution is the stress on an inculturated theology. By "inculturation" is understood the incarnation of evangelical life and the evangelical message in and through members of a particular culture, in such a way that Christian experience is expressed not only in terms of that culture (that would be a simple adaptation), but so that it becomes a force that inspires culture, gives direction and effects renewal, thus giving rise to a new reality not only in a particular culture but enriching the universal Church.

Any attempt to create an inculturated theology is challenged by a multifaceted dialogue. Theologians belonging to the local Christian

1

community first enter into dialogue with the living experience of the community to which they belong. Taking this experience as a starting point, they enter into a dialogue with the Christian scriptures, which contain God's revelation in a unique way, but they will also read, at the same time, those wider scriptures of their own tradition. They enter into dialogue with contemporary theologians who have benefited from a dialogue with philosophers, scientists, psychologists, etc. and at the same time they will try to enter into dialogue with researchers in similar fields belonging to they own culture. These theologians might also benefit from entering into dialogue with the patristic writings. These are a large corpus of inculturated theology. Indeed, many patristic writings convey an implicit answer to the question: "How to express the Christian faith and experience when entering a new culture?" In many different ways, patristic theologians tried to express this faith and experience in the language of the Greek or Latin culture to which they belonged.

Anyone attempting inculturation in Chinese culture might not only benefit from reading the Church fathers, he or she might also benefit from reading the writings of the 17th century Chinese Christians. For these writings also convey an implicit answer to the question: "How to express the Christian faith and experience when entering Chinese culture?" In many different ways, Chinese Christians tried to express this faith and experience in the language of their time. The answers they gave might not be completely appropriate for today. Not only has Chinese culture changed in many aspects, but Christian theology has also undergone considerable changes. However, these Christians faced some fundamental questions that still exist today. Questions like: "Who is God and how can God's name be expressed in Chinese? Why was Jesus Christ not born in China? What is sin and how can it be remitted?" Dialogue with these fundamental questions and with the answers that they gave can be a help for a inculturated theology today.

One should underline some unique characteristics of this collection of writings by Chinese Christians. They were all written by lay people, with only a few works by Chinese who were members of a religious congregation. These lay people were well educated and fully acquainted with their own culture. Some of them had successfully passed the state examinations, while others prepared to do so. Finally, they clearly belonged to a community of Christian faith. Therefore, one could call them theologians, or at least students of theology. In this respect they do not differ that much from many Church fathers who were also lay theologians without a formal training in theology.

Since the author of this dissertation is not of Chinese culture, he will not attempt to formulate an inculturated theology. This dissertation only

2

attempts to collect some fruits from the reflections on the name of God by a 17th century student in theology, called Yan Mo 嚴 謨.

It is divided into two parts. The first part is the translation and analysis of Yan Mo's *Ditiankao* 帝 天 考 [Investigation into the Concepts of Lord and Heaven]. It is preceded by a short biography and bibliography of Yan Mo. In advance it can be pointed out that the *Ditiankao* is historically situated in the term-controversy. Yet, with exception of some historical references, no attempt will be made to analyse the controversy as such. The text was chosen because as such it is of considerable value for a fundamental theological reflection on the name of God in Chinese.

The second part of this dissertation is a further analysis of the concepts of *Tian* and *Shangdi* in the *Book of Documents*, the *Book of Odes*, the *Analects* and the *Mencius*, the major sources used by Yan Mo. In the conclusion there are a few reflections for today on the basis of the analysis done.

Acknowledgments

The study of Christianity in 17th century China has become a highly specialized subject. Due to the vast amount of primary materials and to the dispersion of these materials among libraries all over the world, the detailed study of one figure among the Chinese Christians becomes almost impossible for one person alone. I was lucky to benefit from the help of several people who generously provided me with supplementary information. By name I would like to thank Fr. E. Cerezo S.J. (Taibei), Fr. A. Chan S.J. (San Francisco), Fr. J. De Cock S.J. (Rome), Dra. L. de Lange (Leiden), Dr. N. Golvers (Leuven), Prof. He Zhaowu 何 兆 武 (Beijing), Prof. Huang Yi-long 黃 一 農 (Tsing-hua Univ., Xinzhu), Prof. R. Murray S.J. (London), Fr. L. Morra S.J. (Rome), Ms. Pan Feng-chuan 潘 鳳 娟 (Taibei), Ms. Qian Lingzhu 錢 玲 珠 (Taibei), Dr. C. von Collani (Würzburg), Ms. Zhang Ruiyun 張 瑞 雲 (Taibei), and Prof. E. Zürcher (Leiden). Special thanks are due to Dr. A. Dudink, a long-time colleague, who was also so kind to check the first part of this dissertation. I am grateful especially to Prof. R. Eno (Indiana Univ.) for commenting the chapters on the *Book of Documents* and *Book of Odes*. I also want to thank Frs. P. Brady, F. Conn, and T. Giblin who revised the English at different stages. The mistakes, however, of information and interpretation, should be attributed solely to me.

This study is the revised version of a dissertation presented to the Faculty of Theology of the Fujen Catholic University (Hsin-chuang) in partial fulfillment of the requirements for the degree of Licenciate in Sacred Theology. For generously giving their time to criticize this dissertation as members of the examination committee, I express my appreciation to Prof. Fang Chih-jung S.J. 房 志 榮 (Fujen Cath. Univ., Fac. of Theology), Prof. Fu Pei-jung 傅 佩 榮 (Taiwan Nat. Univ., Fac. of Philosophy), Prof. Ku Wei-ying 古 偉 瀛 (Taiwan Nat. Univ., Fac. of History) and Fr. L. Gendron S.J., Dean of the Faculty of Theology. In addition, I would like to thank Fr. A. A. Roest Crollius S.J. for willing to include this dissertation in the series *Inculturation*.

Finally I want to thank my superiors both in the Society of Jesus and at the Katholieke Universiteit Leuven for giving me the opportunity to conduct this research, as well as my colleagues at the sinological department of the K.U.Leuven, especially Dr. C. Defoort, with whom I had stimulating discussions on the notion of "Heaven".

N.S., Spring 1995.

PART I:

YAN MO AND THE *DITIANKAO*

Chapter 1: Yan Mo

This chapter presents a brief sketch of Yan Mo's life and a list of his writings.

1.1. Yan Mo's life

Very few elements are known about Yan Mo's life 嚴 謨 (*zi*: Dingyou 定 猷; Christian name: Paulus 保 琭 or 保 祿). He was a native of Zhangzhou 漳 州 in Fujian province. The only reference in official Chinese sources is his becoming a Tribute Student (*gongsheng* 貢 生 (*sui* 歲))[1] in 1709 (Kangxi 48) as mentioned in the *Longxi xianzhi* 龍 溪 縣 志 [Local Gazetteer of Longxi District][2]. This information is confirmed by his last available writing, a letter to Father G. Laureati S.J. 利 國 安 (1666-1727) probably written in early 1718.[3]

---

[1] Tribute Student (*gongsheng*) was the designation of students under the Directorate of Education who had been admitted as nominees of local Confucian Schools for advanced study and subsequent admission to the civil service; the *suigongsheng* was one of the several variant references to students annually promoted into the National University at the dynastic capital from local Confucian Schools throughout the empire (Hucker, pp.294-295; p.462).

[2] *Longxi xianzhi* (1762 (Qianlong 27), 1879 (Guangxu)), (*Zhongguo fangzhi congshu* 90), p.174 (j.14, p.28b).; also in *Chongzuan Fujian tongzhi* 重 纂 福 建 通 志 j.166: see Lin Jinshui, p.25 n.4.

[3] Yan Mo, *Zhi Li dalaoye*: first line: 龍 溪 縣 歲 貢 生 嚴 謨.

From his Christian writings we know that he was the son of Yan Zanhua 嚴贊化 (*zi*: Sican 思參; Christian name Ambrosius 盎博削)[4]. Yan Zanhua, himself a Tribute Student by Grace of the year 1651 (*gongsheng, fuxueen* 府學恩)[5] was a fervent Christian belonging to the Fujian community. This information is confirmed by a miraculous event related in the *Annual Letter* of 1649:

> "... From this place [=Anhai] the priest [= Pietro Canevari S.J. (1596-1675)] went away to the city named Chamcheu [=Zhangzhou], which is on the frontier of Cantão [=Guangdong], to which Christians had invited him because they were missing a priest, and since the Tartars robbed everything from the Church of Ciuencheu [=Quanzhou], they brought him some silver and clothes with great love and charity.

> And the priest comments that everyone who contributes to this donation will receive favours from Our Lord, some for themselves, others for their children, as happened to the scholar Ambrosio [=Yan Zanhua], head of the Christian community of Chamcheu [=Zhangzhou], whose son named Paulo [=Yan Mo] fell into the swollen river without being seen, went to the bottom and immediately surfaced again. As soon as the people from home realized the boy was missing, they looked for him and saw him on the water, safe and sound, without even having swallowed water. They will all find mercy with the Lord and will be helped as they deserve."[6]

This text seems to indicate that Yan Mo was born in the mid 1640s.

Yan Mo's father was a disciple and collaborator of Guilio Aleni S.J. 艾儒略 (1582-1649) and, among others, he participated in the correction (*dingzheng* 訂正) of the *Kouduo richao* 口鐸日抄 [Daily Record of Oral Preaching] (1630-1640) and the *Lixiu yijian* 勵脩一鑑 [Mirror for Encouragement of Cultivation] (1639), two of the most important writings about activities of Aleni and the Fujian Christian community at the end of the

---

[4] Yan Mo, *Lishi tiaowen*: first line: 閩漳嚴保塿謨定猷氏集答，父嚴盎博削贊化思參氏鑒訂; Fang Hao (1966), p.7 and (1970), p.105, misread his name as Yan Zan 嚴贊 (*zi*: Huasi 化思) and thought they might have been brothers.

[5] *Longxi xianzhi* (1762 (Qianlong 27), 1879 (Guangxu)), (*Zhongguo fangzhi congshu* 90), p.173 (j.14, p.25b); the *fuxue* is the Prefectural school, the state operated Confucian school in a prefectural capital city; *engongsheng* or Tribute Student by Grace, was a status entitling one to participate in the Provincial Examination in the civil service recruitment process and to be considered at least nominally a National University Student under the Directorate of Education, gained by passing a special, irregular recruitment examination (Hucker, p.204, p.217-218).

[6] *Annua da Vice-Provincia da China de 1649*, Ajuda, codex 49-V-13, ff.486r-486v (under "Residencia de Chamcheu, Kimhoa e Ciuencheu'). Information kindly provided by Dra. L. de Lange.

Ming.[7] By the end of the 17th century, however, the organisation of this community had changed quite drastically. The Fujian-province was the center of the Dominican missions in China. In 1706, 25 out their 31 churches in China were located in Fujian. They were joined by the Franciscans and the Fathers of the Missions Etrangères de Paris. The Jesuits on the other hand had reduced their activities in Fujian considerably: in 1694-1697 they only had about eight of their original twenty churches. The catalogues of 1701 and 1703 mention only three Jesuit residences in Fujian.[8]

It seems that the Yan family belonged to the lower literati class. The cover of one of his writings presents Yan Mo as a "litterato Christiano in FuKien".[9] Moreover, in a letter to José Monteiro S.J. 穆 若 瑟 (1646-1720), he mentions that his brother-in-law was participating in the metropolitan examinations (huishi 會 試).[10]

On the basis of Yan Mo's writings we are able to reconstruct several stages in his life quite succinctly. A first collection of writings belongs to the rejection of a text written by the Dominican Father Francisco Varo 萬 濟 國 (1627-1687) entitled Bianji 辯 祭 [Arguments against Sacrifices], also called the Fuan bianji 福 安 辯 祭 because it was written in collaboration with lower degree-holders (xiushi 秀 士) of Fuan 福 安 (Fujian). It is not clear when the Chinese version of this text was written,[11] but apparently it was rediscovered in an old box by the Jesuit Father Simão Rodrigues 李 西 滿 (1645-1704) in 1681. Rodrigues invited several Chinese to write a criticism of this text.[12] One of those critiques was the Bianji canping 辯 祭 參 評 [Criticism of the Arguments against Sacrifices] by Li Liangjue 李 良 爵, a son of Li Jiugong 李 九 功.[13] It is certain that Yan Mo's father, Yan Zanhua,

---

7 Two of Yan Zanhua's short essays are included in the Tianxue jijie 天 學 集 解 : "Lun fenchu feili" 論 焚 楮 非 禮 (VII, pp.20a-22b) and "Pi lunhui shuo" 闢 輪 迴 說 (VII, pp.23a-26a), cf. Dudink (1993), p.12.
8 Dehergne (1961), pp.326-333.
9 Yan Mo, Jizukao.
10 Yan Mo, Caogao (chaobai), p.1a; also on p.4a in a letter to Fr.Li.
11 Bernard, no.370 gives it the date of 1656, on basis of Biermann, p.211 (22) who writes only "das Buch Pien-Ci = Disputatio de Sacrificio" without giving a date; Varo is well-known for his Vocabulario de la lingua mandarina..., but he also wrote treatises related to the Chinese Rites: Respuesta a las apologias de los PP. Brancati y Jacobo de Fabre S.J.(at which he worked since 1670) and Tratado en que se ponen los fundamentos que los Religiosos Predicatores tienen para prohibir a sus cristianos algunas ceremonias que los gentiles hacen en veneración de su maestro Confucio y de sus progenitores difuntos... (Fu'an, 1680) (von Collani, p.6): they are partly included in Estratto del trattato circa il culto e le cerimonie de' Chinesi, Coloniae, 1700: The last text in this volume is dated by Varo, December 22, 1681; see Quétif, pp.714-715; see Gonzales (1967), pp.37-60; see also Gonzales (1955) (information provided by Dudink and von Collani).
12 See Lin Jinshui, p.25.
13 Ibidem; Jap.Sin.I [38/42] 40/5; it is quite sure that Li Liangjue is Leontius or Leantius Li Yifen 李 奕 芬 who was the catechist and secretary of Maigrot. He accompanied Maigrot to

knew both of them.[14] Yan Zanhua was also involved to some extent in the discussion around the *Bianji*. In 1681, Arcadio del Rosario O.P. (1641-1686) had a conversation with literatus Ambrosius [=Yan Zanhua], who is said to have admitted that he explained the Chinese texts in the same way as Varo did in the *Bianji* before his conversion.[15] Another criticism of Varo's work, entitled *Bianji* 辨 祭 [Discerning Sacrifices], was written by Yan Mo. As a direct response to Rodrigues' request, it cannot be ascertained exactly when it was written, but it dates possibly from the early 1680s. The *Jizukao* 祭 祖 考 [Investigation into Ancestral Worship], the *Muzhukao* 木 主 考 [Investigation into the Ancestral Tablet], *Miaocikao* 廟 祠 考 [Investigation into the Ancestral Temple and Shrine] [16] and probably also the *Kaoyi* 考 疑 [Investigation into Doubts][17] most likely date from the same period.

The second period of writing follows the Edict of Charles Maigrot, Vicar Apostolic of Fujian, member of the Paris Foreign Mission Society. On March 26, 1693, Maigrot issued a mandate to the priests of his vicariate forbidding the Jesuits' missionary practice with regard to the rites, without ever once mentioning the Jesuits by name. Maigrot's mandate caused sensation, anger, and division in China and enormous interest in the church circles of Europe. As a result of it, in 1697, the Pope ordered the Holy Office to reopen the whole question of the Chinese Rites. Hence, it is often considered as the real start of the Rites Controversy. Maigrot's text contains seven articles, two of which are worth quoting in order to better understand the context of Yan Mo's writings:

"Art.1. Leaving out the European names which cannot be expressed in Chinese except in some barbarism, we decree that God should be called *Tien Chu* [*Tianzhu*, Master of Heaven], a name established by long usages. Two older Chinese words--*Tien* [*Tian*, Heaven], and *Xang Ti* [*Shangdi*, High Lord]--should be avoided completely. Let no one say that what the Chinese understand by these words--*Tien* and *Xang Ti*--is the God whom we Christians worship."

Beijing in December 1706 and complained to the Kangxi Emperor that Maigrot was not a devoted student but that he only believed what Father Van (Varo) had said (information provided by Dudink).

[14] Yan Zanhua worked with Li Jiugong on the redaction of the *Kouduo richao* and the *Lixiu yijian*; he also wrote a preface to Li Jiugong's *Shensilu* 慎 思 錄 (Courant 7227-7229; Jap.Sin. I 34/37,1; Bernard, 442) .which was edited by Li Yifen around 1681.

[15] Biermann, p.171 n.59.

[16] In Jap.Sin.I [38/42] 41/1 these two works are bound together with the *Bianji*. The cover bears an inscription in Latin: "Libellus de examine/ oblationis rite orationes illarum/ quae colen fieri in oblatio/nibus, item tabulae quae defunctis/ ponitur rite discursus de litera çi/ contra Pe. Varro ordinis Praedica/ factus a Jen Paulo litterato Christ./ a FuKien." At the end of the other version of the *Bianji* (Jap.Sin.I [38/42] 40/6a) reference is made to the *Muzhukao* .

[17] Mentioned at the end of both versions of the *Bianji*, it was written prior to the *Bianji*.

"Art.4. On no account are missionaries to allow Christians to preside at, to serve, or to be present at the solemn sacrifices or oblations they are in the habit of offering to Confucius and their ancestors several times a year. We say these offerings are tainted with superstition."[18]

This decree seems to have had a serious impact on the community in Zhangzhou. Christians were refused sacraments because they followed the teachings of the Jesuits and objected to Maigrot's edict. A collective letter seeking Monteiro's help by six Christians, including Yan Mo, dates from this period. To this letter is added the *Bianji houzhi* 辯 祭 後 誌 [Post-scriptum to the *Arguments against Sacrifices*], which is dated autumn 1695. There was also a further letter to Monteiro and a letter to a certain Fr. Li, in which it said the Christians were refused confession for one year. These most probably date from the same period.[19] The last letter has attached corrections to the *Lishi tiaowen* 李 師 條 問 [Successive Questions of Fr.Li] originally written "one year" earlier. It seems that as a result of Maigrot's edict, Jesuits had started to ask for additional reference material from their followers among the Chinese Christians. The *Lishi tiaowen* answers in great detail about thirty such questions concerning sacrifices, oblations and Confucius' rituals. Because of Yan Mo's earlier relationship with S. Rodrigues, it is not impossible that Rodrigues is the Father Li to whom the text is addressed. Another letter to Monteiro, the *Zhi Mu dalaoshi wen ershou bayu yishou* 致 穆 大 老 師 文 二 首 跋 語 一 首 [Two Pieces of Text and One Post-Scriptum Addressed to Father Monteiro], equally includes some primary source material concerning rituals, and might date from this period as well.

There are a few writings, such as the *Cunpupian* 存 璞 篇 [To Preserve the Unpolished], the *Shishu bian cuojie* 詩 書 辨 錯 解 [Discussing the Misinterpretation of the *Book of Odes* and the *Book of Documents*] and the *Ditiankao* 帝 天 考 [Investigation into the concepts of Heaven and Lord], whose date is difficult to establish. They might date from the period following Maigrot's decree, but could also be situated in the period preceding it (for further discussion of the date of the *Ditiankao*, see next chapter).

We do not know very much about the later stages of Yan Mo's life. As mentioned, he became a Tribute Student in 1709. In his last letter dated around 1718, he relates that he had been looked after by the Jesuits since his youth and that he was by then an old man ("in his eighties" 耋). From this letter it appears that even at the end of his life he did not cease to defend Church matters and to encourage the Jesuits to take action.

---

[18] See Noll, p.9.
[19] In Yan Mo, *Caogao (chaobai)*, p.4a.

It seems that all his life "he was very loyal to the Jesuits and a strenuous defender of the Chinese Church". As far as his Chinese is concerned, "he has a good style: logical, clear and vigorous".[20]

[20] Comments made by A. Chan in a letter to the author (January 4, 1991).

1.2. Yan Mo's writings

Bianji 辨祭 [Discerning Sacrifices]

    a) Jap.Sin.I [38/42] 40/6a: 11 pages/ 8 col./ 24 char.[21]
    b) Jap.Sin.I [38/42] 41/1c: 6 fols./ 9 col./ 24 char.

    Discernment about what are sacrifices in response to F. Varo's (1627-
        1687) (萬濟國) *Bianji* 辨祭 [Arguments against Sacrifices].

    The two versions are slightly different (in choice of words). At the
    end of the first text reference is made to the *Muzhukao*. The
    second version is bound together with the *Jizukao* and the first
    version of the *Muzhukao*. At the end of both texts a reference is
    made to the *Kaoyi*. At the end of the second text, the author
    explains to the unidentified addressee that he no longer has a
    copy of the *Kaoyi*, but that Luo 羅 and Li 李 in the capital have a
    copy that could be duplicated.[22]

Bianji houzhi 辨祭後誌 [Post-scriptum to the *Arguments against Sac-rifices*]

    Jap.Sin.I [38/42] 41/2b: 3 fols./ 10 col./ 28 char.

    At the beginning of the text, Yan Mo says that he formerly wrote a
    Bianji in response to Varo's text, but since [嚴] 默覺 (= his
    nephew) is now proclaiming the same ideas as Varo, he made
    additional explanations. The text is dated 1695 (autumn month),
    which indicates that the *Bianji* itself is earlier than this date. The
    text is added to the *Caogao*.

Caogao 草稿 [A Rough Draft]

    Jap.Sin.I [38/42] 41/2a: 2 fols./ 10 col./ 29 char.

    Caogao is the title on the cover: it includes a letter and the *Bianji
    houzhi*.

---

[21] "Jap.Sin." refers to a collection in the Jesuit Archives, Rome.
[22] The *Kaoyi* is earlier than the *Bianji*, it was probably composed in the early 1680s. Li might well be S.Rodrigues who was in Zhangzhou for some time and who left in 1679 for Beijing (in 1682 back in Fujian); cf. Dehergne (1973), p.203; it is not clear whether Luo is G.Lopez O.P.

Letter by Yan Mo together with five other Chinese Christians to José
Monteiro (1646-1720) (穆若瑟 mentioned as 穆大老師)[23] to
seek his help. He and others have been accused by Fr. Ma 馬 (=
Maginus Ventallol O.P. 馬喜諾 (1647-1732))[24] of committing
mortal sins, because of his writings against Varo and his refusal to
accept Charles Maigrot's (顏 [璫] 主敎) decision. They are not
allowed to have confession. Yan's nephew 默覺 is ill and wants
to have confession. This is refused unless he writes a retraction of
his involvement in Yan Mo's writings. Since this retraction might
be used by the Dominicans and Missions Etrangères de Paris
against Yan Mo, the latter wrote the *Bianji houzhi* to state his view
more strongly.

Caogao (chaobai) 草稿 (抄白)[A Rough Draft (copy)]

Jap.Sin.I [38/42] 41/4: 12 fols./ 9 col./ 26 char.

Caogao (chaobai) is the title on the cover. On the cover it is also
requested to send the text to Li. It includes several documents: a
letter to Monteiro, table of contents of *Li laoshi tiaowen* (in
which are mentioned *Jizu, Muzhu, Miaocikao* and *Bianji, Kaoyi*),
a letter to Li (? = S.Rodrigues) and two revised answers already
contained in the *Lishi tiaowen*. In the letters the conflict with
Maigrot is mentioned. Reference is also made to Fr. Nie 聶 (= 聶
仲遷 Adrien Grelon (1618-1696))[25] in Jiangxi. In the letter to
Li, mention is made of the confession conflict; moreover it is said
that the *Laoshi tiaowen* was written in the "previous year"
(Monteiro has a copy of it) but it was now revised.

---

[23] Monteiro was appointed vicar de vara of Fujian, 1687-1693; it seems that he was also
Jesuit superior in Fujian in 1695; cf. Dehergne, p.179; Colombel, II p.426.
[24] Biography: *Sinica Franciscana* III p.594 n.7; he was at that time in Zhangzhou: *Sinica
Franciscana* V p,263; Colombel II, p.461; Ventallol wrote *Authenticum Instrumentum
declarationis factue tam suo quam aliorum ejusdem Ordinis Missionariorum nomine, Confucii
et progenitorum cultum Sinensium improbatum a nostris semper fuisse, et etiam nunc
improbari, nec unquam nostros sententiam mutasse, - Datum Focheu, 16 Dec. 1691*, included
in *Apologie des Dominicains*, pp.173-177; cf. González (1967), p.73; Streit, V, p.953.
[25] Grelon was in Jiangxi (with a short interruption) from 1687 till his death in 1696; he was
interested in the question of rites: see Courant 7157: 禮記祭禮泡製 : "Cet ouvrage,
incomplet, avait été rédigé à Khien-tcheou par Hia Ma-ti-ya [= 夏相公 ; cf. Lin Jinshui,
p.26] pour aider le P.Grelon dans ses travaux; écrit en 1698 [?]"; cf. Jap.Sin. I (38/42) 39/4..

16

Cunpupian 存璞篇 [To Preserve the Unpolished]

Borgia Cinese 316.6.a: 11 fols./ 9 col./ 22 char.[26]

This is an anonymous writing. In Hou Wailu (p.1220: based on another version?)[27] it is attributed to Yan Mo. It is a rejection of the Song interpretation of concepts like *shangdi, tian, miao* (shrine) etc... Because of its contents, and because it is addressed to the Greatest Father (太老師: the pope?) and to the fathers of all religious orders, it might well be written by Yan Mo.

On the cover is written in Italian: "Methodo di conservar la sincerita". It is bound together with a writing entitled *Yuanlilun* (see "Other writings").

Ditiankao 帝天考 [Investigation into the Concepts of Lord and Heaven]

a) R.G.Oriente III 248 (10): 20 fols./ 8 col./ 24 char.[28]
b) Borgia Cinese 316.9: 14 fols./ 9 col./ 24 char.

For a complete description see next section of this dissertation. The second version is bound together with the *Miaocikao*.

Jizukao 祭祖考 [Investigation into Ancestral Worship]

Jap.Sin.I [38/42] 41/1a: 11 fols./ 9 col./ 24 char.

Research into the ancestral worship: the original meaning, the ritual during the period of the Three Dynasties, the *Family Rituals* of the Song Confucians, etc., based on many quotations from Classical works. Bound together with the second version of the *Bianji* and the first version of the *Muzhukao*.

---

[26] "Borgia Cinese" refers to a collection in the Vatican Archives.
[27] In Hou Wailu it is mentioned as *Cunpubian*: 存朴編.
[28] "R.G.Oriente" refers to a collection in the Vatican Archives.

Kaoyi 考 疑 [Investigation into Doubts]

Jap.Sin.I [38/42] 40/6b: 15 pages/ 9 col./ 27 char.

Discussion with regard to ancestral worship (seeking happiness, coming to eat...)

The work seems to be earlier than the *Bianji*. The original text is presented to an anonymous addressee. At the end it is said that Luo 羅 and Ou 歐 already had the book which they copied to send it to Wan 萬 and Xia 夏.[29]

Lishi tiaowen 李 師 條 問 [Successive Questions of Fr.Li]

a) Jap.Sin.I [38/42] 40/2: 100 pages/ 8 col./ 24 char.
b) Borgia Cinese 316.10: 49 fols./ 8 col./ 24 char.

Very systematic work in which questions raised by Fr. Li are answered on basis of Classical writings (of which a list is given at the beginning of the text). At the beginning it is mentioned that the answers were collected by Paul Yan Mo, while his father Ambrosius Yan Zanhua made the corrections: 閩漳嚴保琭謨定猷氏集答，父嚴盎博削贊化思參氏鑒訂.

The two versions have the same contents, but there is a different arrangement of the questions. The first version includes a copy of the *Muzhukao*.

Miaocikao 廟 祠 考 [Investigation into the Ancestral Temple and Shrine]

Borgia Cinese 316.9 (b): 4 fols./ 9 col./ 22 char.

Title on first page: *Zongmiao citang kao* 宗 廟 祠 堂 考. This is an anonymous work but it must be of Yan Mo: because it is bound together with the *Ditiankao*. Moreover, on the cover it is written: "can be bound after the *Muzhukao*"; also it is mentioned together with the *Muzhukao* and others in the *Caogao (chaobai)*. It is based on the same concept as the *Jizukao* and *Muzhukao*.

---

[29] It is not impossible that these are all non-Jesuits: Luo = Lopez; Ou = del Rosario; Wan = Varo; Xia: unidentified.

18

Muzhukao 木主考 [Investigation into the Ancestral Tablet]

> a) Jap.Sin.I [38/42] 41/1b: 4 fols./ 9 col./ 24 char.
> b) Jap.Sin.I [38/42] 40/2: 8 pages/ 8 col./ 24 char.

> Historical investigation into the meaning of the ancestral tablet (in a way similar to the *Jizukao*). The second version is slightly different from the first (it occupies pp. 93-100 of *Lishi tiaowen*). The first version is bound together with the *Jizukao* and the second version of the *Bianji*.

Renlei zhen'an xu 人類真安序 [Preface to the True Peace of the Human Race]

> Xu Jiahui Library 410

> Preface to a work composed by 歐加略 (= Arcadio del Rosario O.P. (1641-1686)), probably dated 1700.[30]

Shishu bian cuojie 詩書辨錯解 [Discussing the Misinterpretation of the *Book of Odes* and the *Book of Documents*]

> Reference to this work is made at the end of the *Ditiankao*, but until now it has not been located (not in Paris B.N., British Museum, Petrograd, Rome (National Library, ARSI, Vatican Library), Oxford (Bodleian)). It is quoted in Hou Wailu, p.1216, 1220. This section, where Yan Mo is considered to be a Jesuit, was written by He Zhaowu 何兆武 who based his research on the material gathered by Xiang Da 向達 during his trip in Europe in the 1930s. These copies were, however, destroyed during the Cultural Revolution [31]

> Since it is mentioned at the end of the *Ditiankao*, therefore it is earlier than the *Ditiankao*.

---

[30] Xu, p.427: 題人類真安稿; also Chen Yuan, vol.I, p.114; the author is indebted to A. Dudink for this reference.

[31] Information provided by Prof. He Zhaowu in a letter to the author (June 4, 1992).

Tiandikao 天 帝 考 [Investigation into the Concepts of Heaven and Lord]

see *Ditiankao*

Zhi Li dalaoye 致 利 大 老 爺 [Letter to Father G.Laureati]

Jap.Sin. 178: Sina Epistola, 1718-1720 Folio 35.

In this letter Yan Mo asks the Jesuits to take action against the possible publication of the *Longxi xianzhi* 龍 溪 縣 志 in the manuscript version of which Christianity is described as an heterodoxy (under section 風 俗, written by Chen Yuanlin 陳 元 麟). This event happened in the last month of the year (1717). Yan Mo calls himself 龍 溪 縣 歲 貢 生 (Tribute Student). G.Laureati 利 國 安 (1666-1727) sent this letter to visitator K.Stumpf (1665-1720) on 23 April 1718.

Zhi Mu dalaoshi wen ershou bayu yishou 致 穆 大 老 師 文 二 首 跋 語 一 首 [Two Pieces of Text and One Post-Scriptum Addressed to Father Monteiro]

Jap.Sin.I [38/42] 41/3: 6 fols./ 10 col./ 28 char.

Collection of two primary source materials sent as a reference to Monteiro with the request to send a copy of it to Fr. Nie 聶 (A. Grelon) in Jiangxi (who had already written a text about the topic).

Zhouyi zhiyi 周 易 指 疑

Not located yet but mentioned in Hou Wailu, p.1220 (see *Shishu bian cuojie*).

Other writings:

It is not impossible that some other anonymous writings were originally compiled by Yan Mo:

Jizu yuanyi 祭 祖 原 意 [The Original Meaning of Ancestral Worship]

> Borgia Cinese 316.11: 45 pages/ 8 col./ 21 char.

> This work has the same lay-out as the *Lishi tiaowen* (Borgia Cinese 316.10) and discusses the Ancestral Worship on the basis of Chinese Classical writings. It is followed by a post-scriptum (跋 語) on pp.40-45. The text that immediately follows it (pp.46-96) enlists quotations from the Classics on a great variety of subjects (among others: *muzhu*, *tian*, *shangdi*, etc.). It might belong to the same author.

Yuanlilun 原 禮 論 [Discussion of the Original Rites]

> Borgia Cinese 316.6.b: 4 fols./ 10 col./ 28 char.

> This work is bound together with the *Cunpupian*. The contents correspond to Yan Mo's other writings.

Chapter 2: The *Ditiankao*

This chapter contains a presentation of Yan Mo's *Ditiankao* 帝 天 考 [Investigation into the concepts of Lord and Heaven]. It analyses the two different versions that are preserved. Moreover it attempts to answer questions concerning the title and the date of the text.

2.1. Versions

There are two versions of the *Ditiankao*, which we will call "version A" and "version B".

Version A.: Bibliotheca Apostolica Vaticana R.G. Oriente III 248 (10): 20 fols./ 8 col./ 24 char.

This version is reproduced in Wu Xiangxiang 吳 相 湘 (ed.), *Zhongguo shixue congshu* 中 國 史 學 叢 書 [Collection on Chinese History], no.40: *Tianzhujiao dongchuan wenxian xubian* 天 主 教 東 傳 文 獻 續 編 [Second Collection of Documents on the Spread of Catholicism in the East], Taibei, 1966, vol.1, pp.49-92. The quality of the reproduction (or of the original) is not very good.

On the cover is written in Chinese ...*kao* 考 and in Latin: "*Huius scripti scopus totus est in affirmare et probare* tian *et* sciang ti *esse Dei Sacrum, quem nos Christiani colimus. Ideoque...err...cus tal... et per const.....tus.*" [The purpose of this writing consists completely of affirming and proving that *tian* and *sciang ti* are devoted to God (or: are the sacred of God), which we Christians, venerate. And therefore, ...].[1]

Version B: Borgia Cinese 316.9: 13 fols./ 9 col./ 24 char.

On the cover is written in Chinese *Ditiankao* and in Italian: "Definizione di Dio".

The quality of this text is very good. Due to the different arrangement of the characters, it occupies less folios than Version A. However, the address (cf. Version A, p.51) is missing.

2.2. Title

There is some uncertainty about the title of this work. Until now it was known as *Tiandikao* 天 帝 考, the title used by Fang Hao for the photo-reproduction of the text.[2] The reproduction of the cover, however, only has the character *kao* and this corresponds to the present state of the original text.[3] Moreover, version B has *Ditiankao* 帝 天 考 both on the cover and on the first page . Pelliot's catalogue of the Vatican Library mentions *Ditiankao* as well.[4] Finally, in the text itself *di* and *tian* also appear in this order.[5] For all these reasons it seems more likely that the original title of the text was *Ditiankao*, which will be adopted in this dissertation.

2.3. Date

The address, which is only found in version A, is an important element in establishing the date of the composition of the work. In this address the text is sent to 費, while he is asked to transmit it for reference to

---

[1] The author is indebted to Dr.N. Golvers for his help with the transcription of this very corrupted text; according to Pelliot (p.105) this text was written by Carolus Orazi de Castorano (1673-1755).

[2] Fang Hao does not mention where he got the title; he might have taken it from the Latin description which mentions first *tian*, then *sciang ti*.

[3] The author is indebted to L. Morra for his help with comparing the reproduction with the original text; the cover of the original has several holes so that in the reproduction characters of the next page appear.

[4] Pelliot, pp.24, 105, 112: *Ti t'ien kao* (for both version A and B).

[5] Yan Mo, *Ditiankao*, p.53 first line: 言 上 帝 言 天; p.80, sixth line: 言 上 帝 言 天 之 語 以 備 參 考; the expression 天 帝, meaning "Emperor of Heaven" is confusing; it might still be that version A had this expression in the title, but that it was changed by Yan Mo in version B.

24

羅 萬 南 魯 畢 聶 李 in various provinces. Fei is called *dalaoshi* 大 老 師 while the others are simply called *shi* 師.

Fang Hao 方 豪 was the first one who tried to rediscover the names of the persons involved. Working on the supposition that Yan Mo was a Late Ming figure, he identified Luo as João da Rocha 羅 儒 望 (1565-1623), Li as Manuel Dias 李 瑪 諾 senior (1559-1639) and Nie as Pietro Canevari 聶 伯 多 (1586-1675). As a result, he thought that the *Ditiankao* was a very early writing since da Rocha had already died in 1623. The other names, however, could not be identified by Fang Hao.[6] Since Fang Hao did not know that Yan Mo was a figure of a much later period, his proposal cannot be maintained.

Recently, Huang Yilong 黃 一 農 made new attempt at identification.[7] His starting point is the difference between the terms *dalaoshi* and *shi*. The term should refer to a person with a higher position (in the Church structure). Among the Jesuits from the earlier period who have the surname Fei, no one seems to have held a position to be called Fei *dalaoshi*: Gaspar Ferreira 費 奇 規 (1571-1649), Rui de Figueiredo 費 樂 德 (1594-1642), Francisco Ferreira 費 藏 裕 (1604-1652), Luis de Figueiredo 費 類 思 (1622-1705) and Ehrenbert Xav. Fridelli 費 隱 (1673-1743). One possibility, however, is the name of Filippo Fieschi or Flisco (1636-1697) who held the position of Visitor of the Chinese Vice-province of the Society of Jesus in the period July-October 1697. Fieschi's Chinese name is not known but his name could indeed be Fei. In that case, as Huang Yilong indicates, the *Ditiankao* was finished by the year 1697. The advantage of this suggestion is that it dates the work after Maigrot's decree. The remark at the end of the *Ditiankao* goes in the same direction: "I am concerned about the fact that among the priests who newly arrived there are some who did not do any investigation but they consider the name of 'High Lord' as heterodox. Restrained by their worries, they forbid its appellation and falsely accuse the ancient saints and sages of our country for not knowing the 'Master of Heaven'".[8] Yet, the weak point in Huang's argumentation is that it is impossible to identify the seven other names. These might not necessarily be Jesuits (in that case even Fei might not necessarily be a Jesuit)[9].

Here we would like to argue that the *Ditiankao* possibly dates from the 1680s, even if a final proof could not be found. The starting point in this

---

[6] Fang Hao (1966), pp.7-8; Fang Hao (1970), pp.105-106; Fang Hao misread 畢 as 羅.
[7] Huang Yilong, pp.7-8; the author is grateful to Prof. Huang Yilong for having shared his valuable material.
[8] Yan Mo, *Ditiankao*, pp.91-92.
[9] Moreover one would expect Yan Mo certainly to send a copy to Monteiro, who was the leading Jesuit figure in Fujian by that time but whose name is not mentioned in Yan Mo's list of addressees.

analysis is the list of the seven names. A first presupposition is that the seven names are all, or nearly all, Jesuits.[10]

Because Yan Mo's particular relationship with Nie in Jiangxi, Nie is probably Adrien Grelon 聶 仲 遷 (1618-1696).[11] Li can possibly be identified as Simão Rodrigues 李 西 滿 who suggested that Yan Mo write a criticism of Varo's *Bianji*.[12] The other names would then possibly be (in order of certainty): Ferdinand Verbiest 南 懷 仁 (1623-1688), Giandomenico Gabiani 畢 嘉 (1623-1694)[13], Miguel de Irigoyen 魯 日 孟 (1646-1699)[14], Paul Banhes Wan 萬 其 淵 (1631-1700), and Alessandro Ciceri (Cicero) 羅 歷 山 (1639-1703)[15].

As for Fei the name of Flisco could still stand since he was provincial of Japan (in Macao) from 1687 till 1690. But it could also be another name for Alessandro (later Francesco Saverio) Filippucci (1632-1692), who was Visitor of Japan and China from 1688 till 1691[16]. Certainly, Filippucci is given the Chinese name 方 (齊 各) 以 智, a name based on his second Christian name Francesco Saverio, but this does not completely exclude the hypothesis that he might as well be known in other regions under the name Fei, which is closer to his surname. Following this hypothesis the text can be dated at the end of the 1680s.

However, the names should not necessarily be limited to Jesuits. The address does not explicitly mention the decree of Maigrot, and does not explicitly divide the missionaries into the "Jesuit position" and the "Dominican position"[17]. So one could also replace some of the doubtful names by Dominicans, who had a close connection with the term controversy

---

[10] In fact, they should not necessarily all be Jesuits; among names mentioned by Yan Mo's other writings, some could not be identified: (cf. Yan Mo, *Kaoyi*).

[11] Since Grelon died in March 1696, it is quite unlikely that Yan Mo would still address his text to him in 1697 as suggested by Huang Yilong.

[12] It could also be 李 明 or Louis-Daniel Le Comte (1655-1728) who left China in 1691.

[13] Gabiani was in Zhangzhou in 1664; as Vice-Provincial (1680-1683; 1689-1993) he was related to the question of the rites in the early 1680s

[14] Irigoyen spent eleven years in China, part of which in Fuzhou and also in Zhangzhou (1679-1680). Yan Mo might well not have known that he left for Manila in February 1685.

[15] This name is the least sure since Ciceri only spent two years in Canton before leaving abroad for several years. He was appointed visitor of Japan and China in 1689, but was at that time still in Lisbon.

[16] We know of Filippucci's interest in the rites question since he wrote a work entitled: *De Sinensium politicis acta, seu praeludium ad plenam disquisitionem de cultu Confucii et defunctorum* (Lyon, 1700) (cf. von Collani, p.20, n.27; von Collani was not yet able to locate this work (letter March 22, 1994)); according to Biermann (p. 211 n.22) this is a response to Varo's *Bianji*; see also Streit V, p.878 and VII, p.10.

[17] This division appears in the later texts of Yan Mo: see Yan Mo, *Caogao*, pp.1a-1b and especially the postscriptum to Yan Mo's *Bianji houzhi* (explicit mention of Dominicans and Jesuits); see also Yan Mo, *Caogao (chaobai)*, pp.1a-1b.

or who happened to have stayed in Zhangzhou. Suggestions for these names are made by Dr. A. Dudink.[18]

Wan and Luo might well be Francisco Varo O.P. 萬 濟 國 (1627-1687), the author of the *Bianji*, and Gregorio Lopez O.P. 羅 文 藻 (1611-1690)[19]. Moreover, Fei might well be Pedro de Alcalá O.P. 費 理 伯 (1640-1705), who was *vicarius provincialis* of the Dominicans in China from May 1682 till May 1688.[20] Under this hypothesis, the text was probably written in the first half of the 1680s, possibly 1684 or earlier, because at that moment everybody was present: Besides Varo and Lopez, Verbiest, Irigoyen (left for Manila in February 1685), Grelon, Gabiani (in Fuzhou, 1682) and Rodrigues. Fei might still refer to Filippucci who was provincial of Japan (December 1680 - December 1883).

This data enables one to reconstruct the possible historical context of the text. Zhangzhou was a Jesuit mission since 1635. However, there was no priest living there anymore from 1651, as a result of which the local Christian community, which was composed of more than a hundred families, wrote letters of complaint. Yet, the community was still visited from time to time: by Gabiani in 1664 and Irigoyen in 1679-1680.[21] Around 1680, Zhangzhou was placed under the responsibility of the Dominicans: Varo allowed Lopez to buy a house which was converted into a church by Pedro de Alcalá. In the first years of the 1680s, Arcadio del Rosario was active in the environment of Zhangzhou as well.[22]

At that time, there seems to have been a lot of discussion concerning the question of rites among the Dominicans and Jesuits in Fujian, especially in Zhangzhou. For instance, Lopez wrote a treatise on the rites question in Zhangzhou in December 1681.[23] In the same year, as mentioned earlier, Arcadio del Rosario had a conversation with Ambrosius Yan Zanhua, Yan Mo's father, about Varo's treatise on the rites (*Bianji*), the Western version of which was also finished in 1681. Yan Zanhua is said to have admitted that before his conversion he explained the Chinese texts in the same way as Varo did in the *Bianji*.[24] At the same time (December 1681), Yan Mo and others, under the encouragement of Rodrigues, responded with a refutation of

---

[18] The author is grateful to Dr. A. Dudink for having shared his material (letter of March 1, 1994).
[19] Besides Lopez involvement in the terms controversy, he also stayed in Zhangzhou for some time: he bought a house in Zhangzhou which was converted into a Church by P. de Alcalá (Dehergne (1961), p.331).
[20] *Sinica Franciscana* VIII 2, pp.767, 1006.
[21] Dehergne (1957), p.23; (1961), p.331; (1973), p.130.
[22] Biermann, p.136.
[23] Streit, V, p.896; the text was translated into Latin in 1686 and the French version was included in *Apologie des Dominicains*, pp.366-373.
[24] Biermann, p.171 n.59.

Bianji. Filippucci, who wrote a Latin refutation of Varo's text, and Alcalá[25] were also involved in the discussions. Although the opinions were divided, on the whole it seems to have been a rather "open discussion" : Yan Mo seems to have sent his texts to Jesuits and Dominicans alike. The tone of the discussion was to become quite different after Maigrot's mandate which implied the refusal of the sacrament of confession for many members of the Christian community of Zhangzhou.

It is not impossible that still in the early 1680s the "newly arrived priests" (Rosario, and possibly Alcalá) raised the question whether or not the Chinese Classics speak about God (*Tianzhu*). They might well have taken a position that was different from the interpretation that the local Christians used to hear from the Jesuits. In response, Yan Mo prepared a defense and composed the *Ditiankao*. Like his other writings, he submitted it for discussion to those directly or indirectly involved in this controversy: Father Fei (Filippucci, Jesuit provincial or Alcalá, vice-provincial of the Dominicans and superior of the Dominicans in Zhangzhou), and also to Lopez, Varo, Verbiest, Irigoyen (the last Jesuit priest in Zhangzhou) and Rodrigues. This seems to be the background and network of people involved in the minor rites and terms controversy at a local level around 1682. From this it also appears that Yan Mo was a very prolific writer at that time.

2.4. Arrangement of the text

The text can be divided into three parts:

1) The address (only present in version A).

2) The list of 65 quotations from the *Book of Documents, Book of Odes* and the *Four Books* that mention the terms "High Lord" and "Heaven". We will call this section *List of Quotations*.

3) The *Personal Discussion* in addendum (*fu yulun* 附 愚 論). Here Yan Mo cites a large number of phrases taken from the quotations cited in the second part. In addition there are more than 14 new quotations.

As for the *List of Quotations*, the origin of the quotations is divided as follows:

---

[25] In 1680, Alcalá wrote a letter to P. Intorcetta S.J. (1625-1696) which later became the object of a small controversy since Alcalá is said to have supported the Jesuit position in this letter; it appears that Alcalá had an open position around 1680; cf. Streit, V, pp.872, 916; *Apologie des Dominicains*, pp.398-413.

1 -33: *Book of Documents* (33 quotations)
34-59: *Book of Odes* (26 quotations)
60-61: *The Analects* (2 quotations)
62   : *Doctrine of the Mean* (1 quotation)
63-65: *Mencius* (3 quotations)

For each quotation, three different annotations are given:

a) The reference of the book or the section of the book from which the quotation is taken.

b) The comment which usually consists of two parts: the explanation of some difficult characters and a paraphrase of the quotation. This section is usually taken from the Song commentaries on these writings:

> *Book of Documents*: *Shu(jing) jizhuan* 書〔經〕集傳 by Cai Chen 蔡 沈 (1167-1230) (preface 1209).
> *Book of Odes*: *Shi(jing) jizhuan* 詩〔經〕集傳 by Zhu Xi 朱 熹 (1130-1200) (preface 1177).
> *Four Books*: *Sishu jizhu* 四書集注 by Zhu Xi (1177).

The comment given by Yan Mo is only a selection of Song commentaries, since his original quotations belong to a large group of characters on which the Song scholars gave a more extensive annotation. In most cases, Yan Mo's selection is literal, although some differences exist (see below).

c) The context from which the quotation is taken. Usually Yan Mo indicates who originally said the quotation. Sometimes the author adds his own paraphrase.

The following two quotations may serve as an example of his way of annotation:

[4] 天敘有典，天秩有禮，天命有德，天討有罪

From Heaven are the arrangements with their several duties; from Heaven are the distinctions with their several ceremonies; Heaven graciously distinguishes the virtuous; Heaven punishes the guilty.

a) See Gaoyaomo 皋 陶 謨.[26]

b) *Xu* 敘 means the social order between sovereign and minister, father and son, elder and younger brother, husband and wife, and between friends; *zhi* 秩 means the hierarchical order between honorable and mean, noble and mean, higher and lower ranks, abundant and restrained. Heaven distinguishes people who are virtuous and Heaven punishes people who are guilty.[27]

c) Here Gaoyao told Yu that the sovereign among men completely depends on Heaven for the duties, ceremonies, distinctions and punishments.

[8] 有 夏 多 罪 ， 天 命 殛 之 ， 予 畏 上 帝 ， 不 敢 不 正

For the many crimes of the sovereign of Xia, Heaven has given the charge to destroy him. As I fear the High Lord, I dare not but punish him.

a) See Tangshi 湯 誓.[28]

b) Jie of Xia was cruel. Heaven ordered to destroy him. Since I fear the High Lord, I dare not but go and punish his crimes.[29]

c) These are the words of the speech of Tang of Shang when he was about to assault Xia.

2.5. Difference between versions A and B

In general, the differences between the two texts are very small. Taking the *Personal Discussion* as an example, one can mainly find the following differences:

- the different writing of a character or a group of characters: 于 (A) = 於 (B); 妙 (A) = 玅 (B); 蕩 、 (A) = 蕩 蕩 (B), etc.;

- the omission of certain characters by version B: 尚 書 詩 經 及 四 書 instead of 尚 書 詩 經 二 經 及 四 子 書 (A); 祥 殃 instead of 百 祥 百 殃 (A);

---

[26] This is the title of one of the chapters of the *Shujing*: Gaoyaomo (4), pp.73-74.

[27] Literally taken from *Shujing jizhuan*, p.17 (some parts are left out since the quotation is itself also a selection).

[28] This is the title of one of the chapters of the *Shujing*: Tangshi (10), pp.173-174.

[29] Literally taken from *Shujing jizhuan*, p.43.

- the addition of certain characters by version B: 四 子 書 instead of 四 子 (A); 答 曰 instead of 曰 (A).

None of these differences have any serious influence on the text. They do not enable us to determine the original text. Even the more important differences, which will be pointed out in analysis of the text, do not enable us to make a conclusive argument. There are, however, reasons to consider version A as being earlier than version B. The main reason is the differences that appear between the two versions in the second part of the annotations (those copied from the Song authors). *In every case in which there is a difference between the two versions, version A is closer to the original Song commentary than version B.* It is rather unlikely that version B had changed the quotation and that this was later corrected according to the original by version A. One rather should opt for the solution that version B made some minor changes while copying from version A. The following examples illustrate these differences[30]:

In the annotation [4] (see translation above) version A is: 敘 者 君 臣 父 子 兄 弟 夫 婦 朋 友 之 倫 敘 也. This is taken literally from the *Shujing jizhuan*.[31] Version B has made a minor change: 敘 者 君 臣 父 子 兄 弟 夫 婦 朋 友 五 倫 之 敘 也.

In the annotation [14] version A is: 不 常 者 去 就 無 定 也. This is again taken literally from the *Shujing jizhuan*.[32] Version B only writes: 不 常 無 定 也.

In the annotation [15] of version A one finds, following the *Shujing jizhuan*[33]: 是, 古 是 字 。 。 。 湯 常 目 在 是 天 之 明 命. Version B has changed the second 是 into 此.

In the annotation [18] of version A, it is written, in correspondence with the *Shujing jizhuan*[34]: ...夢 帝 與 我 以 賢 輔; version B has 良 instead of 賢, since 良 also appears in the quotation of the *Shujing*.

Two additional arguments would point to version A as more original: a) the fact that version A has an address and that at the end of the personal discussion it maintains a greater formality in the lay-out than version B; b)

---

[30] For other examples see: [5], [9], [12], [13], [14] (at the end), [25], [33], [35], [37], [46], [47], etc.; only the third difference (addition of 爭) in [9] is closer to the *Shujing jizhuan*, but this change could occur without reference to this commentary since the character already appears before; the difference in [17] is not necessarily based on the *Shujing jizhuan*.

[31] *Shujing jizhuan*, p.17.

[32] *Shujing jizhuan*, p.48.

[33] *Shujing jizhuan*, p.49.

[34] *Shujing jizhuan*, p.58.

the fact that in version B of the *Personal Discussion*, there are more characters added (30) than omitted (21).

However, there are some reasons to believe that the copy was made by someone close to Yan Mo, if not by Yan Mo himself. As in the case of other writings, Yan Mo had several copies of his text sent to different fathers, who in turn might have copied the text. In the case of these two versions of the *Ditiankao*, it seems quite likely that a copy was made with some direct link to Yan Mo and that the copyist, probably Yan Mo, consciously made some changes to the first version. This supposition can be deduced from the following two examples:

For [26], version B has a shorter quotation from the *Book of Documents* than version A (予 一 人 恭 行 天 罰 is omitted), but the corresponding commentary from the *Shujing jizhuan* is also omitted.

For [61] one has the inverse case: the quotation from the *Analects* in version B is longer than in version A (小 人 不 知 天 命 而 不 畏 也 is added), but the corresponding commentary from the *Sishu jizhu* is also added.

These changes could only have been made by someone well acquainted with the subject.

As a conclusion of this section, we will use version A as a reference (also because it is more easily available due to its photo-reproduction), but when it is necessary, we will also refer to version B.

Chapter 3: Translation

This chapter presents a translation of *List of Quotations* and the *Personal Discussion* as they appear in the Yan Mo's *Ditiankao*.

3.1. List of Quotations

This section contains a translation of the 65 quotations taken from the Classical writings. The translation is based on the translations by Kalgren and Legge. Since most of Yan Mo's comments are rather technical in nature, they have not been translated. However, a special section is devoted to their analysis in the next chapter. The underlined sections (in Chinese) or sections in italics (in English) are quoted in the *Personal Discussion*.

[1] 肆 類 于 上 帝

Shundian (2), p.33.

Thereafter, he offered special sacrifice, but with the ordinary forms, to the High Lord.[1]

---

[1] Also in Yan Mo, *Cunpupian*, p.3a,2.

[2] 皇天眷命，奄有四海，爲天下君

> Dayumo (3), p.54.

> *Great Heaven regarded you with its favouring decree, and suddenly you obtained all within the four seas, and became sovereign of the empire.*

[3] 天之曆數在汝躬

> Dayumo (3), p.61.

> *The determinate appointment of Heaven rests on your person.*

[4] 天敘有典 [...] 天秩有禮 [...] 天命有德 [...] 天討有罪

> Gaoyaomo (4), pp.73-74.

> Heaven arranges the existing rules [...] Heaven regulates the existing rites [...] *Heaven gives charges to those who have virtue* [...] *Heaven punishes those who have guilt.*[2]

[5] 以昭受上帝，天其申命用休

> Yiji (5), p.79

> *And you will brightly receive gifts from Heaven; will not Heaven renew its favouring appointment and give you blessing?*[3]

[6] 敕天之命惟時惟幾

> Yiji (5), p.89.

> *Being charged with the favourable appointment of Heaven, we must be careful at every moment and in the smallest particular.*

---

[2] Also in *Tianzhu shiyi*, p.530,8 (343).
[3] Also in Yan Mo, *Cunpupian*, p.3a,2.

[7] 天 用 勦 絶 其 命 [...] 今 予 惟 恭 行 天 之 罰

Ganshi (7), p.153.

Heaven therefore cuts off his appointment. [...] Now I furnish and practise Heaven's punishment.

[8] 有 夏 多 罪 ， 天 命 殛 之 [...] 予 畏 上 帝 ， 不 敢 不 正

Tangshi (10), pp.173-174.

For the many crimes of the sovereign of Xia, *Heaven has given the charge to destroy him.* [...] As I fear the High Lord, I dare not but punish him.[4]

[9] 惟 天 生 民 ， 有 欲 ， 無 主 乃 亂 。 惟 天 生 聰 明 時 乂

Zhonghuizhigao (11), pp.177-178.

Heaven gives birth to the people with such desires, that without a ruler they must fall into all disorders. And *Heaven again gives birth to the man of intelligence* whose business is to regulate them.

[10] 夏 王 有 罪 ， 矯 誣 上 天 。 [...] 帝 用 不 臧 ， 式 商 受 命 。 [...] 欽 崇 天 道 ， 永 保 天 命 。

Zhonghuizhigao (11), p.179, 183.

The king of Xia was an offender, *falsely pretending* to the sanction of High Heaven. [...] On this account, the Lord viewed him with disapprobation, caused [our] Shang to receive his appointment. [...] To revere and honour the way of Heaven is the way to always preserve the favouring decree of Heaven.

[11] 惟 皇 上 帝 降 衷 于 下 民 ， 若 有 恆 性 ， 克 惟 綏 厥 猷 惟 后

Tanggao (12), p.185.

The Great High Lord *has conferred [even] on the inferior people a moral sense,* compliance with which would show their nature

---

[4] Also in *Tianzhu shiyi*, p.416,3 (108); second part also in Yan Mo, *Cunpupian*, p.3a,3.

invariably right. [But to] cause them tranquilly to pursue their course which it would indicate, is the work of the sovereign.[5]

[12] 天道福善禍淫，降災于夏，以彰厥罪

Tanggao (12), p.186.

The way of Heaven is *to bless the good and to punish the bad. It sent down calamities on [the House] of Xia*, to make manifest its crimes.

[13] 爾友善，朕弗敢蔽，罪當朕躬，弗敢自赦，惟簡在上帝之心

Tanggao (12), p.189.

The good in you, I will not dare to conceal; and for the evil in me, I will not dare to forgive myself; I will examine these things in harmony with the mind of the High Lord.

[14] 惟上帝不常，作善降之百祥，作不善降之百殃

Yixun (13), p.198.

[The ways] of the High Lord are not invariable; *on the good-doer he sends down all blessings, and on the evil-doer he sends down all miseries.*

[15] 先王顧諟天之明命 [...] 天監厥德，用集大命

Taijia (*shang*) (14), p.199.

The former king kept his eyes continually on the bright requirements of Heaven. [...] Heaven took notice of his virtue and caused its great appointment to light on him.

---

[5] Also in Yan Mo, *Cunpupian*, p.3a,3 and in *Tianzhu shiyi*, p.416,4 (108).

[16] 惟 天 無 親 ， 克 敬 惟 親

　　　Taijia (*xia*) (16), p.209.

　　　Heaven *has no affection*, only on those who are reverent does it show affection.

[17] 天 難 諶 ， 命 靡 常 [...] 夏 王 弗 克 庸 德 [...] 皇 天 弗 保 監 於 萬 方 ， 眷 求 一 德 [...] 克 享 天 心 受 天 明 命 非 天 私 我 有 商 ， 惟 天 祐 於 一 德

　　　Xianyouyide (17), pp.213-216.

　　　It is difficult to rely on Heaven, its appointments are not constant. [...] The king of Xia could not maintain the virtue [of his ancestors] unchanged [...] Great Heaven no [longer] *extended its protection* to him. It looked out among the myriad regions to give its guidance to one who might receive its favour, *fondly seeking* a [possessor] of pure virtue, [...] *able to satisfy the mind of Heaven* and to receive [in consequence] the bright favour of Heaven. [...] It was not that Heaven had any partiality for the ruler of Shang, Heaven simply gave its favor to pure virtue.

[18] 恭 默 思 道 ， 夢 帝 賚 予 良 弼

　　　Yueming (*shang*) (21), p.250.

　　　While I was respectfully and silently thinking of the [right] way, I dreamt that the Lord gave me a good assistant.

[19] 惟 天 聰 明 ， 惟 賢 時 憲 [6]

　　　Yueming (*zhong*) (22), p.255.

　　　It is Heaven which is *all-intelligent and observing*. Let the sage [king] take it as his pattern.

---

[6] 賢 should be read 聖.

[20] 惟天監下民，典厥義，降年有永有不永。非天夭民，民中絕命

Gaozongrongri (24), p.264.

When Heaven inspects the people below, it takes as norm their righteousness and sends down life either long or not long. It is not that Heaven prematurely kills the people, the people in the middle cut off their lives.

[21] 皇天震怒，命我文考，肅將天威

Taishi (*shang*) (27), p.285.

Great Heaven *was moved with indignation*, and charged my deceased father Wen reverently to display its majesty.

[22] 乃夷居，弗事上帝，神祇

Taishi (*shang*) (27), p.286.

He abides squatting on his heels, not serving the High Lord or the spirits of heaven and earth.

[23] 天祐下民，作之君，作之師，惟其克相上帝寵綏四方

Taishi (*shang*) (27), p.286.

Heaven, *to protect* the inferior people, *made for them rulers and made for them instructors*, that they might be able to aid the High Lord, and secure the tranquillity of the four quarters of the empire.

[24] 商罪貫盈，天命誅之，予弗順天，厥罪惟鈞

Taishi (*shang*) (27), p.287.

The iniquity of Shang is full. Heaven gives command to destroy it. If I did not comply with Heaven, my iniquity would be as great.

[25] 天矜于民，民之所欲，天必從之

Taishi (*shang*) (27), p.288.

Heaven compassionates the people. What the people desire, Heaven will be found to give effect to.

[26] 上帝弗順，祝降時喪 [...] 予一人，恭行天罰 [7]

Taishi (*xia*) (29), p.295-296.

The High Lord will no longer indulge him, but determinedly *is sending down* on him this ruin. [...] I, the one man, reverently execute the punishment appointed by Heaven.

[27] 予小子敢祇承上帝，以遏亂略

Wucheng (31), p.313.

I, who am but a little child, [...] presume reverently to comply with [the will] of the High Lord, to make an end of his disorderly ways.

[28] 惟天陰騭下民，相協厥居

Hongfan (32), p.320.

Heaven *shelters* and raises the people here below, it *aids* and harmonizes its dwelling.

[29] 鯀 [...] 汩陳 [其] 五行，帝乃震怒，不畀洪範九疇，彝倫攸斁 [...] 禹 [乃] 嗣興，天 [乃] 錫禹洪範九疇，彝倫攸敘

Hongfan (32), p.323.

Gun [...] brought disorder into the arrangement of the five elements. *The Lord then was roused to anger*, and did not give him the Great Plan in nine sections, whereby the constant norms were destroyed. [...] Yu [then] succeeded him and rose. *Heaven [then] gave Yu* the Great Plan, whereby the constant norms get their proper order.

---

[7] The second part of this sentence is not quoted by version B.

[30] 乃 命 于 帝 庭 ， 敷 佑 四 方

Jinteng (34), p.354-355.

But he has been appointed in the Lord's hall, extensively to possess the regions of the earth here below.[8]

[31] 予 惟 小 子 ， [不][9] 敢 替 上 帝 命

Dagao (35), p.369.

I, little child, dare not find fault with the command of the High Lord.

[32] 文 王 克 明 德 [...] 聞 于 上 帝 ， *帝 休* ， 天 乃 *大 命* ， 文 王 ， 殪 戎 殷 ， 誕 受 厥 命

Kanggao (37), p.383, 385.

King Wen was able to make bright the virtue [...] and it was heard by the High Lord, and *the Lord favoured him*. Heaven then *grandly ordered* king Wen to *kill the great Yin* and grandly to receive its mandate.

[33] 皇 天 上 帝 改 厥 元 子 ， 茲 大 國 殷 之 命 ， 惟 王 受 命 ， 無 疆 惟 休 ， 亦 無 疆 惟 恤

Shaogao (40), p.425.

Oh, August Heaven, High Lord, has changed his principal son and this great state Yin's mandate. Now that the king has received the mandate, unbounded is the grace, but also unbounded is the solicitude.

---

[8] Also in *Tianzhu shiyi*, p.416,5 (108).
[9] Version A has not the negation; this is corrected in version B.

[34] 帝命不違，至于湯齊，湯降不遲，聖敬日躋，昭假遲遲，上帝是祗，帝命式于九圍

Ode 304,3. (p.640)

The Lord's commands were never disobeyed; all down to Tang they were all alike; Tang came down not late; *his wisdom and reverence daily advanced; brightly he advanced steadily;* the High Lord, him he revered; *the Lord charged him to be a model to the nine regions.*[10]

[35] 皇矣上帝，臨下有赫，監觀四方，求民之莫 [...] 上帝耆之，憎其事廓

Ode 241,1. (pp.448-449)

August is the High Lord, looking down, he is majestic; he inspected and regarded the [states of] the four quarters, *he sought tranquillity for the people.* [...] The High Lord brought it to a settlement, *he enlarged their measurements [of the boundaries].*

[36] 帝遷明德

Ode 241,2. (p.450)

The Lord transferred the bright virtue.

[37] 帝省其山 [...] 帝作邦作對[11]

Ode 241,3. (pp.450-451)

The Lord examined the mountains. [...] The Lord *made* a state and *made* a counterpart of himself.

---

[10] Also in *Tianzhu shiyi*, p.415,8 (105).
[11] The original text and version B have 對 instead of 對.

[38] 維 此 王 季 ， <u>帝 度 其 心</u> ， 貊 其 德 音 [...] 既 受 帝 祉 ， 施 于 孫 子

    Ode 241,4. (pp.451-452)

Now this king Ji, the Lord probed his heart; *settled was his reputation*, in his virtue he was able to be enlightened. [...] He received the Lord's blessing; it reached to his grandsons and sons.

[39] 帝 <u>謂</u> 文 王 ， 無 然 畔 援 ， 無 然 歆 羨 ， 誕 先 登 于 岸

    Ode 241,5. (p.452)

The Lord *said* to king Wen: "Do not like that be relaxed, do not like that indulge your desires." And so he ascended a high bank.

[40] 帝 <u>謂</u> 文 王 ， 予 懷 明 德 不 識 不 知 ， <u>順 帝 之 則</u>

    Ode 241,7. (p.454)

The Lord *said* to king Wen: "I think cherishingly of your bright virtue. [...] Without [the need of] knowledge or wisdom, *you follow the patterns of the Lord*."

[41] 其 香 始 升 ， 上 帝 居 歆 [...] 后 稷 肇 祀 ， 庶 無 罪 悔 ， 以 迄 于 今

    Ode 245,8. (p.472)

As soon as the fragrance ascends, the High Lord tranquilly enjoys it. [...] Hou Ji initiated the sacrifice, and the multitude has given no offense nor cause for regret unto the present day.

[42] 文 王 在 上 ， 於 昭 于 天 [...] 文 王 <u>陟 降</u> ， 在 帝 左 右

    Ode 235,1. (pp.427-428)

King Wen is on high. Oh! bright is he in Heaven. [...] King Wen ascends and descends, he is on the left and the right of the Lord.[12]

---

[12] Also in *Tianzhu shiyi*, p.551,9 (391).

[43] 上帝既命，侯于周服

Ode 235,4. (p.430)

When the High Lord gave his appointment, they became subject to Zhou.

[44] 上天之載，無聲無臭

Ode 235,7. (p.431)

The actions of High Heaven have no sound, no smell.

[45] 維此文王，小心翼翼，昭事上帝

Ode 236,3. (p.433)

Now this King Wen, *he was careful and reverent; brightly he served the High Lord.*[13]

[46] 上帝臨女，無貳爾心

Ode 236,7. (p.436)

The High Lord is with you, do not be double-minded in your heart.

[47] 我將我享，維羊維牛，維天其右之 [...] 我其夙夜，畏天之威，于時保之

Ode 272,1.3. (pp.575-576)

I present my offerings, there are sheep, there are oxen; may Heaven esteem them. [...] May I night and day fear the majesty of Heaven, and thereby preserve it.

---

[13] Also in *Tianzhu shiyi*, p.415,9 (105); p.556,2 (406) (=Chinese scholar) and p.589,7 (483).

[48] 時 邁 其 邦 ， 昊 天 其 子 之

Ode 273,1. (p.577)

He makes his seasonal tour in his state; may Heaven cherish him as a son.

[49] 不 顯 成 康 ， <u>上 帝 是 皇</u>

Ode 274,1. (p.578)

Greatly illustrious were Cheng and Kang, *the High Lord made them sovereigns.*[14]

[50] <u>敬 之 敬 之</u> ， 天 維 顯 思 ， 命 不 易 哉 ， 無 曰 高 高 在 上 ， 陟 降 厥 士 ， 日 監 在 茲

Ode 288,1. (pp.598-599)

Be reverent, be reverent, Heaven is splendid, its charge is not easy; do not say "It is very high above"; *it ascends and descends in our workings, and daily inspects us who are here.*

[51] 明 昭 上 帝 ， 迄 用 康 年

Ode 276,3. (pp.582-583)

Bright is the High Lord, it has come to our having a happy year.[15]

[52] 受 祿 于 天 ， <u>保</u> 右 命 之 ， 自 天 申 之

Ode 249,1. (p.481)

He receives his dignity from Heaven, it *protects*, helps and appoints him, by repeated acts of renewal from Heaven.

---

[14] Also in *Tianzhu shiyi*, p.415,7 (105).
[15] Also in *Tianzhu shiyi*, p.415,8 (105).

[53] 上帝板板，下民卒癉

Ode 254,1. (p.499)

The High Lord has become stern, and the lower people are full of distress.

[54] 敬天之怒，無敢戲豫，敬天之渝，無敢馳驅，昊天曰明，及爾出王，昊天曰旦，及爾游衍

Ode 254,8 (p.503)

Revere the anger of Heaven, dare not play and enjoy yourselves; revere the changing moods of Heaven, dare not race about; Great Heaven is called intelligent, *it is with you in all your doings*; Great Heaven is called clear-seeing; *it observes your wanderings and extravagances.*

[55] 蕩蕩上帝，下民之辟

Ode 255,1. (p.505)

How vast is the High Lord, he is the ruler of the people below.

[56] 昊天上帝，則不我遺

Ode 258,3. (p.530)

Great Heaven High Lord does not let us survive,

[57] 天生烝民，有物有則，民之秉彝，好是懿德

Ode 260,1. (p.541)

Heaven gave birth to the multitude of people, they have *things*, they have *rules*; that the people hold on to the norms is because they have that beautiful virtue.

[58] 民 今 方 殆 ， 視 天 夢 夢 ， 既 克 有 定 ， 靡 人 弗 勝 ， 有 皇 上 帝 ， 伊 誰 云 憎

> Ode 192,4. (p.316)

> The people are now in peril, *they look on Heaven as undiscerning;* but let its determination be fixed, and *there is none whom it will not overcome, the August High Lord,* whom does he hate?

[59] 藐 冒 昊 天 ， 無 不 克 鞏

> Ode 264,7. (p.564)

> The distant Great Heaven, *is able to strengthen anything.*

[60] 獲 罪 於 天 ， 無 所 禱 也

> *Analects* III,13.

> *He who offends against Heaven has none to whom he can pray.*[16]

[61] 君 子 [...] 畏 天 [小 人 不 知 天 命 而 畏 也][17]

> *Analects* XVI,8.

> The superior man [...] stands in awe of the decree of Heaven; [the mean man does not know the decree of Heaven and [consequently] does not stand in awe of it].

[62] 郊 社 之 禮 ， 所 以 事 上 帝 也

> *Doctrine of the Mean* 19.

> By the ceremonies of the sacrifices to Heaven and Earth, they served the High Lord.[18]

---

[16] Also in *Tianzhu shiyi*, p.468,5 (206).
[17] The second part is added by version B.
[18] Also in *Tianzhu shiyi*, p.415,5 (104).

[63] 存 其 心 ， 養 其 性 ， 所 以 事 天 也

Mencius VII A,1.

To preserve one's heart, to nourish one's nature, is the way to serve Heaven.

[64] 莫 非 命 也 ， 順 受 其 正

Mencius VII A,2.

There is an appointment for everything; obey by receiving {the appointment] proper {to you].

[65] 雖 有 惡 人 ， 齊 戒 沐 浴 則 可 以 祀 上 帝

Mencius IV B,24.

Though a man may be wicked, yet if he adjust his thought, fast and cleanse himself, he may sacrifice to the High Lord.

3.2. Personal Discussion

[80] **[7b]**[19] In addition a *Personal Discussion*.

{1} Among the ancient books of my country China, only the sayings of the *Five Classics* and the *Four Books*[20] are reliable. Yet, the *Yijing* discusses symbols[21], but does not concretely talk about things; the *Annals of Spring and Autumn* on their side record the human affairs from the end of the Zhou, while the *Book of Rites* is for the larger part a writing dating from the Qin and Han dynasty. Only what is recorded in the two Classics, the *Book of Documents* and the *Book of Odes* and in the *Four Books* **[8a]** is detailed and their words are without falsehood. Now, one wants to know what is meant by *Shangdi*. Therefore, I carefully selected and recorded the expressions concerning *Shangdi* and *Tian* as mentioned in the two Classics and the *Four Books*, to be used as reference.

{2a} According to the present research, [it can be concluded that] the ancient Chinese expression *Shangdi* is precisely [the same as] the Western expression *Tianzhu*.

"He is great" (惟 皇)[22] and **[81]** "he is august" (皇 矣)[23], these expressions mean that he has no equal in respect.

He is called "vast" (蕩 丶)[24] and "wide" (浩 丶)[25] which means that his substance is inexhaustible.

One says that "the actions of High Heaven have no sound, no smell" (上 天 之 載 ， 無 聲 無 臭)[26], it means that he is purely spiritual without form.

---

[19] The numbers between bold brackets refer to the page number of the original text: the number 80+ refer to version A (according to the page number of the reprint in the *Tianzhujiao dongchuan wenxian xubian*); the number 7b+ to version B.

[20] The author uses the expression *sizi* 四 子 "four masters"; version B writes *sizishu* 四 子 書 ; as appears further in the text, this expression should be understood as the *Four Books*.

[21] *xiang* 象 this is a reference to the *sixiang* 四 象 produced by *yin* and *yang*.

[22] [11] (= reference number in *List of Quotations*) = Tanggao (12), p.185.

[23] [35] = ode 241,1.

[24] [55] = ode 255,1.

[25] = ode 194,1; not cited in Yan Mo's *List of Quotations*.

[26] [44] = ode 235,7.

And it is also said that "the appointment of Heaven, oh, is august and never-ending" (維天之命，於穆不已)[27], he is indeed without end.

It is said that "it is with you in all your doings" (及爾出往)[28] and that "it observes your wanderings and extravagances" (及爾游衍)[29] and that "it ascends and descends in our workings and daily inspects us who are here" (陟降厥事，日監在茲)[30], this all means that there is nothing he does not know and there is nowhere where he is not present.[31]

"It is able to strengthen anything" (無不克鞏)[32] and "there is none whom it will not overcome" (靡人弗勝)[33]: nothing is impossible to him.

It is said that "he is majestic" (有赫)[34], "he is splendid" (顯思)[35], "all-intelligent and observing" (聰明)[36], "moved with indignation" (震怒)[37], indeed he is intelligent and powerful.

It "sees and hears" (視聽)[38], "graciously favours" (眷祐)[39], "gives and protects" (錫保)[40], "inspects and regards" (監觀)[41], "shelters and aids" (陰相)[42], "looks down" (臨下)[43], it "has no affection" (無親)[44], "is not constant" (靡常)[45], "makes" (作)[46], "sends down" (降)[47], "compassionates"

[27] = ode 267; not cited in Yan Mo's *List of Quotations*.
[28] [54] = ode 254,8; 往 should be read 王.
[29] ibidem.
[30] [50] = ode 288,1; 事 should be read 土.
[31] In the translation of the following sentences, "it" refers to the description of Heaven in the Chinese Classics, "he" to the description of the Christian God.
[32] [59] = ode 264,7.
[33] [58] = ode 192,4.
[34] [35] = ode 241,1.
[35] [50] = ode 288,1.
[36] [19] = Yueming (*zhong*) (22), p.255.
[37] [21] = Taishi (*shang*) (27), p.285.
[38] Taishi (*zhong*) (28), p.292; not cited in Yan Mo's List of Quotations.
[39] Taijia (*zhong*) (15), p.206; Weizizhiming (36), p.378; 佑 instead of 祐; not cited in Yan Mo's *List of Quotations*; however in [17] = Xianyouyide (17), p.214-216 and separately in [2] = Dayumo (3), p.54 and in [23] = Taishi (*shang*) (27), p.286.
[40] Separately in [29] = Hongfan (32), p.323; [17] = Xianyouyide (17), p.214; [52] = ode 249,1.
[41] [35] = ode 241,1.
[42] [28] = ode 241,4.
[43] [35] = ode 241,1.
[44] [16] = Taijia (*xia*) (16), p.209.
[45] [17] = Xianyouyide (17), p.213.
[46] [23] = Taishi (*shang*) (27), p.286; also [37] = ode 241,3.
[47] [26] = Taishi (*xia*) (29), p.295.

(矜)[48] and "speaks" (謂)[49]: indeed, he is supreme spiritual [8b] and supreme living.

It "gave birth to the multitude of people" (生烝民)[50] and "has conferred on the inferior people a moral sense" (降衷于下民)[51]: indeed, he gave birth to the human being and its nature.

"It blesses the good and punishes the bad" (福善禍淫)[52], "it gives charges to those who have virtue and punishes those who have guilt" (命有德，討有罪)[53] and "on the good-doer it sends down all blessings, and on the evil-doer it sends down all miseries" (作善降之百祥，作不善降之百殃)[54]: [82] these expressions mean that he likes the good and hates evil, that he rewards the good and punishes the bad.

Where it is said that "Heaven compassionates the people" (天矜於民)[55], that it "seeks tranquillity for the people" (求民之莫)[56], that "Heaven has given the charge to destroy him" (天命殛之)[57] and that "it sends down calamities on the [house of] Xia" (降災于下)[58], it means that he is supreme benevolent and supreme righteous.

Those who follow [Heaven][59], become saints and sages, as it is said that "forever he was worthy of [Heaven's] appointment" (永言配命)[60], "he was able to satisfy the mind of Heaven" (克享天心)[61] and "follow the patterns of the Lord" (順帝之則)[62].

Those who go against [Heaven][63], become mean people, as it is said that they "falsely pretended [to the sanction of Heaven] and committed many crimes" (矯誣多罪)[64], "their bad fame was plainly felt on high" (穢德升

---

[48] [25] = Taishi (*shang*) (27), p.288.
[49] [39] = ode 241,5 and [40] = ode 241,7..
[50] [57] = ode 260,1.
[51] [11] = Tanggao (12), p.185.
[52] [12] = Tanggao (12), p.186.
[53] [4] = Gaoyaomo (4), p.74.
[54] [14] = Yixun (13), p.198.
[55] [25] = Taishi (*shang*) (27), p.288.
[56] [35] = ode 241,1.
[57] [8] = Tangshi (10), p.173.
[58] [12] = Tanggao (12), p.186; 下 should be read 夏.
[59] This is a paraphrase of *Mencius* IV A,7: 順天者存.
[60] = ode 235,6 and 243,2; not cited in Yan Mo's *List of Quotations*.
[61] [17] = Xianyouyide (17), p.215.
[62] [40] = ode 241,7.
[63] This is a paraphrase of *Mencius* IV A,7: 逆天者亡.
[64] first part [10] = Zhonghuizhigao (11), p.179; second part [8] = Tangshi (10), p.173.

聞)[65] and that they "did not know and did not stand in awe [of Heaven]" (不知 不 畏)[66].

{2b} Therefore, one has to observe throughout history the teaching of how the ancient saints served Heaven. Regarding this it is said that "being charged with the favouring appointment of Heaven, we must be careful at every moment and in the smallest particular" (敕 天 之 命 ， 惟 時 惟 幾)[67], and that "his wisdom and reverence daily advanced, brightly he advanced steadily" (聖 敬 日 躋 ， 昭 格 遲 、)[68] and "he was careful and reverent, brightly he served the High Lord" (小 心 翼 、 ， 昭 事 上 帝)[69]. Furthermore it is said "be reverent, be reverent, Heaven is splendid" (敬 之 敬 之 ， 天 維 顯 思)[70] and "he who offends against Heaven has none to whom he can pray" (獲 罪 於 天 ， 無 所 禱 也)[71] and "to preserve the heart and to nourish the nature is the way to serve Heaven" (存 心 養 性 ， 所 以 事 天)[72]. The learnings of Yao, Shun, Yu, Tang, the Duke of Zhou, Confucius and Mencius were all like this.

Now, among the ancient people in their walkings and doings, there was no one who did not respectfully comply with [the decrees] of the High Lord. [83] [9a] They did so when enthroning, therefore it is said that "the determinate appointment of Heaven rests on your person" (天 之 曆 數 在 爾 躬)[73].

They also did so when appointing officers to fulfill official duties, therefore it is said that "they perform the service of Heaven" (亮 天 功)[74] and that "they act for the work of Heaven" (代 天 工)[75].

They so did as well when performing expulsion and punishment expeditions, therefore it is said that "they carry out the punishment appointed by Heaven" (致 天 之 罰)[76].

---

[65] = Taishi (*zhong*) (28), p.290; not cited in Yan Mo's *List of Quotations*; version B writes 腥 instead of 升 and the original text 彰.

[66] [61] (in version B) = *Analects*.XVI,8.

[67] [6] = Yiji (5), p.89.

[68] [34] = ode 304,3.

[69] [45] = ode 236,3.

[70] [50] = ode 288,1.

[71] [60] = *Analects* III,13.

[72] [63] = *Mencius* VII A,1.

[73] [3] = Dayumo (3), p.61.

[74] = Shundian (2), p.50; not cited in Yan Mo's *List of Quotations*.

[75] = Gaoyaomo (4), p.73; the original text reads: 天 工 人 其 代 之 ; not cited in Yan Mo's *List of Quotations*.

[76] = Tangshi (10), p.175; not cited in Yan Mo's *List of Quotations*.

They also did so when they were afraid that the High Lord would not change what is incorrect, therefore it is said that "the Lord favoured him and grandly ordered him to kill the great Shang" (帝 休 大 命 殪 戎 商)[77].

They respected the [will of] the High Lord so as to stop disorder and to promote every sage, therefore it is said that "Heaven gives charges to those who have virtue" (天 命 有 德)[78], and that "the good in you, I will not dare to conceal, I will examine these things in harmony with the mind of the High Lord" (爾 有 善 朕 弗 敢 蔽 ， 簡 在 上 帝 之 心)[79].

They appealed to the eminent and honorable High Lord so as to punish every crime, therefore it is said that "Heaven punishes those who have guilt" (天 討 有 罪)[80], that "on this account, Heaven is about to destroy him" (天 用 勦 絕 其 命)[81], and that "for the evil in me, I will not dare to forgive myself" (罪 當 朕 躬 ， 弗 敢 自 赦)[82].

They were established as the Sons of Heaven, therefore it is said that "Great Heaven regarded you with its favouring decree, and suddenly you obtained all within the four seas" (皇 天 眷 命 ， 奄 有 四 海)[83], "the Lord charged him to be a model to the nine regions" (帝 命 式 于 九 圍)[84], "[Heaven] made for them rulers and made for them instructors" (作 之 君 作 之 師)[85] and "the High Lord made them sovereigns" (上 帝 是 皇)[86].

They established the country and the capital, therefore it is said that "he enlarged their measurements [of the boundaries], and there gave a settlement" (增 其 式 廓 ， 此 維 與 宅)[87], and "the Lord transferred the bright virtue and examined the mountains" (帝 遷 明 德 ， 帝 省 其 山)[88].

Their heart was virtuous and good, therefore it is said that "[Heaven] gifted the king with valour and wisdom" (錫 王 勇 智)[89], "Heaven gives birth

---

[77] [32] = Kanggao (37), p.385; the original text reads 殷 instead of 商.
[78] [4] = Gaoyaomo (4), p.74; this passage is already quoted above.
[79] [13] = Tanggao (12), p.189.
[80] [4] = Gaoyaomo (4), p.74; this passage is already quoted above.
[81] [7] = Ganshi (7), p.153.
[82] [13] = Tanggao (12), p.189.
[83] [2] = Dayumo (3), p.54.
[84] [34] = ode 304,3.
[85] [23] = Taishi (*shang*) (27), p.286.
[86] [49] = ode 274,1.
[87] [35] = ode 241,1; the second part which is not cited in Yan Mo's *List of Quotations* belongs to the same ode; 憎 is read 增 following Zhu Xi's interpretation.
[88] First part [36] = ode 241,2; second part [37] = ode 241,3.
[89] = Zhonghuizhigao (11), p.178; not cited in Yan Mo's *List of Quotations* but following [9].

to men of intelligence" (天 生 聰 明)[90], [84] "the Lord probed his heart" (帝度 其 心)[91] and "Heaven enlightens the people" (天 之 牖 民)[92].

[Their] affairs were prosperous, therefore it is said that "they brightly receive [gifts from] the High Lord; will he not renew his favouring appointment and give you blessing?" (昭 受 上 帝 ， 申 命 用 休)[93].

In order to guarantee that the appointment is renewed by Heaven,[9b] one necessarily has to make offerings every year, the ritual of which is highly esteemed. And every matter necessarily has to be reported, the feelings of which are very intimate. For disaster and blessings you have to pray, since you know to whom belongs the power; and what you receive has to be requited, since you know who bestows benefits to you. As a result, in all one's doings, in life and death one cannot but say that "one has an appointment [by Heaven]" (有 命)[94] and even in poverty and distress one cannot but say that "one delights in Heaven" (樂 天)[95]. Under a clear sunrise or in dark room, in all places one should be careful of having a moral sense that is honest under all circumstances. In a short instant as well as in early death or long life, at all times one should deepen the learning[96] of acting according to one's nature (率 性)[97] and waiting for what has been appointed (俟 命)[98]. The numerous virtuous actions of all these saints and sages, originated without exception from the fact that they served the High Lord. Therefore there is no doubt that ancient Chinese expression *Shangdi* is precisely [the same] as the Western expression *Tianzhu*.

{3} Someone might object: The Master of Heaven is without beginning and is self-possessing; and in the Master there is the mystery of the Trinity; and the Master of Heaven did the work of creating heaven, earth, the spirits, [85] the human being and the things; until now the [Chinese] books did not mention a word about this[99].

---

[90] [9] = Zhonghuizhigao (11), p.178.
[91] [38] = ode 241,4.
[92] = ode 254,6; not cited in Yan Mo's *List of Quotations*.
[93] [5] = Yiji (5), p.79.
[94] e.g. Yixun (13), p.194; Xianyouyide (17), p.217; ode 236,6; not cited in Yan Mo's *List of Quotations*.
[95] *Mencius* I B,3; not cited in Yan Mo's *List of Quotations*.
[96] Version B has "effort" (功) instead of "learning (學).
[97] *Doctrine of the Mean*, 1.
[98] *Mencius* VII B, 33; also in *Doctrine of the Mean*, 14.
[99] Version B has here a rhetorical question: "...why did [Chinese] books not mention a word about this?"

Hereto [I] answer: the mysteries of the Master of Heaven being without a beginning, and the Trinity, completely surpass human nature. Before the incarnation of the Master of Heaven, [10a] unless it was revealed by the Master of Heaven, people could not know it and did not even dare to talk about it. As for the order of Him creating heaven, earth, the spirits, the human being and things, unless one lived in Judea and was able to read the Ancient Scriptures, one could not know it and did not dare to talk about it. Therefore, that the ancient Chinese saints and sages did not talk about these matters seems appropriate and prudent. One cannot blame them as deficient because of this or argue that the expression High Lord that they use would not be the Master of Heaven.

There are cases where they say that the High Lord is intelligent and powerful[100] and that there is no one higher than him, herein is also contained the meaning of "without beginning".

It is mentioned that "[Heaven] gave birth to the multitude of people" (生 烝 民)[101], that "Heaven gave birth to the people" (天 生 人)[102], "it conferred a moral sense" (降 衷)[103] and "[they have] things and rules" (物 則)[104]; therefore, although it is not said that he created heaven and earth at a given moment, or that he created the human body with clay and put a spiritual nature (soul; 靈 魂) in it, [86] nevertheless one also knew that the High Lord gave birth to the human being and endowed him with a nature[105].

As for the Trinity, one can never attain it.

In spite of this, we are happy that the words of our ancient saints and sages were simple and that their meaning was prudent. The *Analects* say [for example]: "The Master seldom spoke about the appointment [of Heaven]" (子 罕 言 命)[106] and also: "[The Master's] discourses about [man's] nature and the way of Heaven cannot be heard" (性 與 天 道 不 可 得 而 聞 也)[107]. If the words were more numerous, one would inevitably have expressions with an extended meaning or [expressions] which are used as analogies, [10b] and then by chance one might have had one or two expressions which were misleading, so that those who at present discuss the matter, would grasp them [as an argument] not to consider [the High Lord][108] as the Master of Heaven. Should one only start to doubt about words when they become so

---

[100] This is the eight characteristic of God mentioned in section 2a.
[101] [57] = ode 260,1.
[102] [9] = Zhonghuizhigao (11), p.177; read 民 instead of 人.
[103] [11] = Tanggao (12), p.185.
[104] [57] = ode 260,1.
[105] This is the tenth characteristic of God mentioned in section 2a.
[106] *Analects* IX,1; not cited in Yan Mo's *List of Quotations*.
[107] *Analects* V,13; not cited in Yan Mo's *List of Quotations*.
[108] Added in version B.

wicked? If [the Chinese Classics] contained expressions similar to the way in which the Western Ancient Scriptures speak about the Master of Heaven, the High Lord would surely be (falsely) accused of not being the Master of Heaven. Why?

Well, the Ancient Scriptures speak about "God [= Master of Heaven] the Father" and "God [= Master of Heaven] the Son" and record his words "This day I have begotten you"[109]. And it is also recorded that when the Master of Heaven wanted to punish the five cities of Sodom, he said: "I do not trust you, but I look down upon you"[110]. **[87]** Moreover there are images of each person of the Trinity in ancient Western paintings. There are many similar examples. Unless you explain them clearly, [so that one understands that these expressions are used as analogies][111], people will start saying that the Master of Heaven is not at all without a beginning, but that in the Trinity there are the differences between greater and smaller and between earlier and later, [and they will also start saying that] there are things the Master of Heaven does not know and there are places where He is not, and finally that it is not at all the case that He has no form. Then how will you defend yourself? Now, fortunately in our Classics there are no such misleading expressions. Is that not the great advantage of the prudent and simple language of the ancient times?

In the books of other philosophers there are also expressions **[11a]** which are apparently even more clear than those of the *Book of Odes* and the *Book of Documents*. The *Zhuangzi*, for instance, has the expression "creator" (造 物 者)[112] and says "there is a not yet beginning to be a beginning" (有 夫 未 始 夫 有 始 也)[113]. And Laozi says: "there was something undefined and yet complete in itself, born before Heaven-and-Earth" (有 物 混 成 ，先 天 地 生)[114] and "it contained Three which formed One" (函 三 爲 一)[115]. Moreover in Han times people offered to the Three-in-One (三 一)[116]. One

---

[109] Cf. Ps. 2:7; Act. 13:33.

[110] 瑣 法 馬 seems to refer to destruction of Sodom as mentioned in Gen.18-19; in Gen. there is no mention of "five cities"; this expression only occurs in a totally different context in 1 Chr. 4,32 and Lk. 19,19.

[111] Added in version B.

[112] *Zhuangzi* VI,48,49,67,87; VII,9; XXXII,13; XXXIII,67.

[113] *Zhuangzi* II,49; the complete version reads: "There is a not yet beginning to be a not yet beginning to be a beginning" (有 未 始 有 夫 未 始 有 始 也 者).

[114] *Daodejing* 25; translation by John Wu.

[115] This sentence does not belong to the *Daodejing*, the author might have thought of *Daodejing* 14 where it is said that the three attributes (of the Way) fuse into one: 此 三 者 ... 混 而 爲 一. However, the expression appears in the *Hanshu* (Lülizhi (*shang*)), j.20, p.964: 太 極 元 氣 ，函 三 爲 一 where it is explained as "Heaven, Earth and Human Being fusing into one" (天 地 人 混 合 爲 一).

[116] Both in the *Shiji* (Fengshanshu) and in the *Hanshu* (Jiaosizhi) it is mentioned that in ancient times every three years, the Son of Heaven made a great sacrifice to the 三 一: 天 地 太 (泰).

guesses that also in earlier times [similar] expressions were transmitted, but at present I do not dare to quote them as a proof because among them there are too many expressions that are not pure and it is better not to say that they are more appropriate.

{4a} [88] One may again object and say: Since he is called the High Lord, why then is he at some times called Heaven? Heaven, therefore, is certainly not the Master of Heaven.

Hereto I answer: This is a borrowed appellation of people from ancient times. In the Classics he is simply called "Lord" (帝), "High Lord" (上帝), "Great High Lord" (皇 矣 上 帝)[117], "Great and sovereign High Lord" (皇 皇 后 帝)[118], "Vast High Lord" (蕩 蕩 上 帝)[119], these kinds of uncountable expressions of which none belongs to the genre of Heaven. Sometimes he is called "Great Heaven High Lord" (皇 天 上 帝)[120]. This expression is a way to indicate [the name] plainly. Among what human eyes can see, only Heaven is the greatest. By speaking of Heaven one attracts our intelligence to know the greatness of the High Lord. If one only says "Lord", [one should not forget that] the sovereign of man is also called "lord" and without mentioning [11b] "Heaven" it is not sufficient to indicate plainly its greatness.

As for the fact that the Classics occasionally use the single expression "Heaven", this again is a way of using characters. Here the term "Heaven" is borrowed[121] to express "Lord". People today call the Governor of the Metropolitan Prefecture (順 天 知 府) "Metropolitan Prefecture" (順 天 府) [122] and they call a District Magistrate (知 縣) "District" (縣). How could the city by itself be the Governor or the Magistrate? And the Emperor is called "Court" (朝 廷) [89] or "at the lower steps" (階 下). But how could the palace building or the steps by themselves become the most venerable? However, they were borrowed as appellation which point to him. Well, if one can borrow appellations like this for what can be clearly seen among the human race, why could one not borrow the expression of one and great "Heaven"[123] to call the High Lord who is purely spiritual and without a shaped body and as such lead human thought to a place where it can settle. The people of ancient times were also ingenious about this use of characters, and there is

---

[117] [35] = ode 241,1.

[118] = ode 300,3; not cited in Yan Mo's *List of Quotations*.

[119] [55] = ode 255,1.

[120] [33] = Shaogao (40), p.425; only occurrence in the *Book of Documents*; in the *Book of Odes* one finds three times 昊 天 上 帝 in ode 258 (see [56]).

[121] This term (借) is added by version B.

[122] The character 天 is added by version B.

[123] The character 天 is added by version B.

nothing wrong with it. Therefore, when they spoke about "Heaven" it always meant a matter that was intelligent and powerful, it never was that which is contained by the circular body of the firmament and celestial sphere, and they did not worry about it being incomprehensible or confused.

Moreover, it also happens that the Classics use both expressions "High Lord" and "Heaven" in one sentence at the same time. For instance, "You will brightly receive gifts from the High Lord; will not Heaven renew its favouring appointment" (昭 受 上 帝 ， 天 其 申 命)[124], or "falsely pretending to the sanction of High Heaven, on this account the Lord viewed him with disapprobation" (矯 誣 上 天 ， 帝 用 不 臧)[125], [12a] or "the Lord was thereby roused to anger, Heaven gave it to Yu" (帝 乃 震 怒 ， 天 乃 錫 禹)[126] or "they look on Heaven as undiscerning, there is the August High Lord" (視 天 夢 丶 ， 有 皇 上 帝)[127] and so on, we will not detail [them] further; so one should not worry about some people who doubt about the character "Heaven" [90] saying that it cannot point out the High Lord.

{4b} In brief, the Master of Heaven has no name, but because people looked at him, he received a name. The appellations "High Lord" and "Master of Heaven" both express that he is most honorable with no one above him, and that is all, there is nothing strange about it. It is the same as calling the sovereign among men *jun* 君, *hou* 后, *pi* 辟 or *huang* 皇[128]; [these expressions] all refer to one and the same sovereign. And it is the same as calling a father *fu* 父, *ye* 爺 or *qin* 親: they all refer to one and the same father. In fact, one has to look at the meaning of what is referred to. How could one because of the various appellations in different regions say that in that case it is indeed sovereign or father, whereas in this case it is not, and as a result [say] that the "High Lord" is not the "Master of Heaven".

For sure, the two character expression 上 帝 (High Lord) is better than the two character expression 天 主 (Master of Heaven). But it is only considered as appropriate because it certainly resembles to what is called by the West "the ruler of heaven, earth and all things" 天 地 萬 物 之 主 宰. Even if you abbreviate this in the two characters "Master of Heaven", then it is still not more ingenious than the expression "High Lord". Why? Because *di* 帝 means sovereign and *shang* 上 that he is the great sovereign high in Heaven; [91] [12b] it embraces heaven, earth and all things in it. If one calls him Master of Heaven, then people who do not know him, would think that

[124] [5] = Yiji (5), p.79.
[125] [10] = Zhonghuizhigao (11), p.179.
[126] [29] = Hongfan (32), p.323.
[127] [58] = ode 192,4.
[128] Due to a different arrangement of this sentence, version B also adds *zhu* 主 and *di* 帝.

he belongs to Heaven [the sky]. In Han times one also made the distinction between the Master of Heaven 天 主, the Master of Earth 地 主 and the Master of the Mountains 山 主[129], is it not too limited? Moreover, the expression "ruler of heaven, earth and all things" contains too many characters and is difficult to be used as a calling name, therefore there was no alternative but to abbreviate it. If you add a clear explanation, there is no harm in it.

{4c} As for the first priests who came and who translated the scriptures in collaboration with the first generation of Chinese, it was not that they did not know that "High Lord" was the same as "Master of Heaven"; but they continued to call him according to the ancient books. When people saw it, it had already become a common expression. Moreover, Buddhists and Taoists of later generations considered the High Lord as belonging to the human race and as a result his name was considered mean and his position low. When common people heard this name they were not clear about it, therefore following the Western name it was abbreviated into "Master of Heaven". It was not the case that they doubted that in the past "High Lord" did not mean "Master of Heaven" and that therefore they eliminated it and did not dare[130] to use it.

Now, however, I am concerned about the fact that among the priests who newly arrived there are some who did not do any investigation [92] but they consider the name of "High Lord" as heterodox. Restrained by their worries they forbid its appellation[131] and falsely accuse the ancient saints and sages of our country for not knowing the "Master of Heaven". They consider virtuous [13a] and upright people as belonging to the race of rebellious and thieves or followers of devils and demons. The consequence of this misunderstanding will be terrible and will be difficult to detail. Therefore I have recorded carefully what is said in the Classics and added a personal discussion at the end.

However I pray the common mind to eliminate differences and the ascend together to a common excellence in order to conform herein to the will of the Great Master. As for the *Book of Odes* and the *Book of Documents*, the original text is clear but there are a few paragraphs which do

---

[129] Both the *Shiji* (Fengshanshu) j.28, p.1367 (Watson, vol.2, p.24) and *Hanshu* (Jiaosizhi) j.25, p.1202 mention that the First Emperor on a trip to the east, sacrificed to the "famous mountains, great rivers and to the eight gods" (名 山 大 川 及 八 神). The eight gods are named: 天 主, 地 主, 兵 主, 陰 主, 陽 主, 月 主, 日 主, 四 時 主. There is no reference to 山 主; the author might have mistaken it, because of the reference to "famous mountains" in the sentence preceding the description of the eight gods.

[130] The verb "dare" (敢) is added by version B.

[131] Version B writes: "not to name and quote it".

not sufficiently catch the original meaning because of the erroneous interpretation by Later Confucians. I also wrote a booklet entitled *Discussing the Misinterpretation of the* Book of Odes *and* Book of Documents. If someone wants to study it in detail, may he take the trouble to read them.

Compiled and written by Paul Yan Mo Dingyou from Zhang[zhou] in Fujian province.

Chapter 4: Analysis

In this section we will try to analyse Yan Mo's concept of God as it appears in the *Ditiankao*. Our main focus will be his *Personal Discussion*. In order to substantiate and enrich our analysis, we will regularly refer to M. Ricci's *Tianzhu shiyi* 天 主 實 義 [The Solid Meaning of the Master of Heaven]. We do not know whether Yan Mo read the *Tianzhu shiyi*. In his writings we found no reference to a Chinese work of a missionary. However, a man with his cultural background certainly read some of their texts. The *Tianzhu shiyi* was chosen as reference because it was the most famous introduction to the Christian faith in the 17th century. As will appear, it can function as a good contrast. In the second part of this analysis, we will continue our investigation into Yan Mo's idea of God by making a comparison with the writings of the Song Confucianists. Here the focus will be Yan Mo's *List of Quotations*.

4.1. The idea of God in the Personal Discussion

The *Personal Discussion* is divided by the author into four sections which we numbered 1 to 4. In addition we divided section 2 into two sub-sections and section 4 into three sub-sections. In our analysis we will follow this arrangement.

4.1.1. The sources: hermeneutical argument

In the first section, the author gives a hermeneutical statement about his use of sources. He opts for sources whose contents are "reliable" (可 憑). This should be interpreted in the first place as being considered relatively reliable with regard to the ancient times that they discuss. As stated at the beginning of section 2, the author brings out the correspondence between the "ancient Chinese" (古 中) expression *Shangdi* and the Western expression

Tianzhu. Hereto, as stated at the beginning of this section, he bases himself on "ancient writings" (古 書). Although the *Yijing* contains a section on *di*[1], which was quoted among others by Ricci[2], the work is rejected by Yan Mo because it is not concrete enough. As for the discussion of *Shangdi* and *Tian*, the *Annals of Spring and Autumn* and the *Book of Rites* are discarded as well, mainly because they are of recent date. However, they are not rejected as such by Yan Mo. In his writings concerning rites, he often quotes them, especially the *Book of Rites*. There, the *Book of Rites* is described both as a book on "rituals from the period of the Three Dynasties (Xia, Shang, Zhou) and also as compiled by various scholars from the Qin and Han dynasty"[3]. For *Shangdi* and *Tian*, however, he preferred the *Book of Documents*, the *Book of Odes*, and the *Four Books*, because "what they record is detailed and their words are without falsehood". Later in section 3, Yan Mo says that some other writings, such as the *Zhuangzi*, the *Daodejing* and the *Hanshu*, may contain more convincing references, but they are not quoted as a proof because "among them there are too many expressions that are not pure". One can observe that Yan Mo, in the selection of his sources, uses very common commentarial presuppositions, namely that Classics are well ordered and coherent, arranged according to some logical principle, and that they are self-consistent and profound.[4]

Here one should ask whether Yan Mo was aware of the text-history of the books he quoted. From the *Cunpupian* we know that he was clearly aware of the changes these texts underwent. He even attributes the corruption to a demonic influence (魔 鬼). The characteristic of the demon is to deceive the people by drifting along with the prevailing customs and books. All over he throws poison and makes people fall into pitfalls. The *Six Classics* are not exempt from this action. Since the Qin burned so many books, it was easy for Han scholars to change the incomplete texts. Yan Mo continues his argument as follows:

> " The Song scholar Zhu Xi touched the *Book of Documents*
> and sighed emotionally: 'The *Book of Documents* has an Old Text and
> New Text version. The Old Text is the one found in a wall; the New
> text is the one orally transmitted by Fu Sheng 伏 生'[5]. Hereto I say:
> Since the text orally transmitted by Fu Sheng was also an ancient text
> found in a wall, why should one make a difference between the Old Text
> and the New Text Versions? Yet, as for the text that was found in the
> wall, by the time it was found it was necessarily disintegrated [from
> erosion and weathering] and was incomplete. As for the text that was

---

[1] *Yijing (shuogua* IV): 帝 出 乎 震 : "The Lord emerges from Zhen in the East"
[2] *Tianzhu shiyi,* p.416,1 (106).
[3] *Jizukao,* p.1a; *Lishi tiaowen,* p.1a.
[4] Cf. Henderson, esp. p.106, 115, 129.
[5] Cf. Jiang Shanguo, p.276-277; cf. *Zhuzi yulu* 朱 子 語 錄 , j.78.

orally transmitted, when it was recited it was necessarily patched and mended with additions and omissions. One can understand that it was not at all the original text as compiled and corrected by Confucius. If the *Book of Documents* is like this, one can draw analogies for the other books. This is a clear proof of the demon drifting along with prevailing books and throwing poison in them."[6]

As a result Yan Mo calls for an excellent method of eradicating flaws and preserving the unpolished (*cunpu*)[7]. Yan Mo's writings can be considered as an continuous effort to return to the unpolished by eradicating flaws. In Yan Mo's eyes, all classical writings are subjected to this method, because all underwent changes by Han and Song scholars.

By making these hermeneutic remarks at the beginning of his discussion, one already perceives the attention Yan Mo pays to a text as such. There is a clear link between his concept of God and the texts he uses. He is searching for the "unpolished" idea of God as it appears in the early Chinese writings. Therefore he discards unreliable texts that might present a corrupted idea.

4.1.2. Attributes of God: proofs in Chinese Classics

The way the first sentence of section 2 is formulated seems to be of great importance for understanding the position from which the text is written. A comparison with Ricci's *Tianzhu shiyi* is useful. Ricci also tried to show the correspondence between the ideas behind *Shangdi* and *Tianzhu* on the basis of Chinese classical writings. Yet, he was a Westerner (*xishi* 西 士) who addressed himself to a Chinese public (*zhongshi* 中 士). Yan Mo, on the contrary, was a Chinese scholar, who addressed himself to Western missionaries. As a result, Ricci's introductory sentence reads: "Our Master of Heaven is precisely the High Lord as mentioned in the ancient classical writings."[8] In Yan Mo's discussion, the phrase is turned in the other way: "...the ancient Chinese expression High Lord is precisely the same as the Western expression Master of Heaven." This sentence indicates the new hermeneutic situation. We no longer have a foreigner claiming that his God is the same as the one to be found in the Chinese Classics. Here we have a Chinese scholar who was brought up in Chinese tradition and who claims that the notions to be found in this tradition correspond to the Western God in whom he believes.

---

[6] *Cunpupian*, pp.1a-b.
[7] *Cunpupian*, p.1a; see also 7b.
[8] *Tianzhu shiyi*, p.415,4 (104).

Section 2a contains eleven paragraphs in which Yan Mo quotes passages of the Classics which describe God. These are essential for the understanding of his idea of God. The first eight of them describe God *in se*. The last three describe the relationship between God and human beings. The structure of all these paragraphs is the same: the quotations from the Classics (which are excerpts from the *List of Quotations*) precede a short characterization of God. The structure indicates that these attributes are supposed to be the corresponding elements of the "Western" God (*tianzhu*). Indeed, they belong to the common descriptions of God as formulated by the scholastic theology of the missionaries. For instance, nearly all of them appear already formulated as such in the *Tianzhu shiyi*. In total. Yan Mo presents thirteen characteristics:

其 尊 無 對: most venerable without equal[9]
其 體 無 窮: his substance is inexhaustible[10]
純 神 無 形: purely spiritual without form[11]
無 終　　: without end[12]
無 所 不 知: omniscient[13]
無 所 不 在: omnipresent[14]
無 所 不 能: omnipotent[15]
顯 明 威 權: intelligent and powerful[16]
至 神 至 活: supreme spiritual and supreme living
生 人 生 性: gave birth to the human being and its nature[17]
好 善 惡 惡: likes the good and hates evil[18]
賞 善 罰 遏: rewards the good and punishes the bad[19]
至 仁 至 義: supreme benevolent and supreme righteous[20]

At first sight this list seems to be a quite complete description of God. It includes the different attributes of God as formulated by Thomistic theology: the knowledge of God by way of negation ("without form, without end, there is nothing that he does not know"), by way of analogy ("intelligent and powerful") and the perfections of God ("most spiritual, living, benevolent

---

[9] Cf. *Tianzhu shiyi*, pp.392-394 (50-51); p.417,4 (110).
[10] *Tianzhu shiyi*, p.396,5 (55); cf. p.397,7 (60).
[11] *Tianzhu shiyi*, p.398,3 (58) (*shen*); 396,4 (55) (*wuxing*).
[12] *Tianzhu shiyi*, p.389,4 (42); 397,5 (59).
[13] Cf. *Tianzhu shiyi*, p.397,9 (61); 593,6 (493).
[14] *Tianzhu shiyi*, p.593,6 (493); cf. p.397,7 (60); p.398,4 (61); 593,6 (493).
[15] *Tianzhu shiyi*, p.626,3 (574); cf. p.397,9 (61); p.593,6 (493)
[16] *Tianzhu shiyi*, cf. p.410,8 ff (91).
[17] *Tianzhu shiyi*, p.389,9 (44); p.548,3 (383); p.567,6 (432).
[18] *Tianzhu shiyi*, p.445,2 (161); p.549,1 (385).
[19] *Tianzhu shiyi*, cf. p.527,9 (333).
[20] *Tianzhu shiyi*, p.443,3 (157); p.627,1 (576); cf. p.445,2 (161); p.549,1 (385).

and righteous")[21]. Some of these expressions are clear attempts to transpose Western concepts into Chinese and some are difficult to translate back into a Western language because of their multiple meanings in Chinese (e.g. 其 體 無 窮, 神). Others are analogies in which typically Chinese terms for human values (仁, 義) are attributed to God in perfection.

Still, some differences can be observed. The two character combination of 無 終 ("without end") indicates an irregularity within itself. Indeed the normal combination is 無 始 無 終 ("without beginning and without end"). This is a conscious omission. Hence, the absence of 無 始 in the Classical writings is discussed in section 3. In the same line it is mentioned that God gave birth to the human being and to its nature, but the work of creation is omitted. This aspect is also discussed in section 3. One can equally observe that no mention is made of God as *primum mobile*, or of the divine immutability or God as the supreme cause, concepts that were closely related to Western cosmology and philosophy.[22] God being the source of all goodness or love is not really stressed either.[23]

Yan Mo is not the first to have shown the presence of God in the ancient writings and the correspondence with the Christian God. In the *Tianzhu shiyi*, Ricci also included eleven quotations to show this correspondence[24]. But, as far as we know, Yan Mo is the first to have done this in a systematic and nearly exhaustive way. Ricci only quotes eleven sentences one after the other. Yan Mo, on the other hand, sought for the detailed correspondence of each attribute of the Christian God with the excerpts from ancient Chinese writings.

At the end of section 2a, there are two paragraphs with a different structure than the previous ones. They do not describe God, but the relationship between the human being and God or better the effect of this relationship: those who follow God become saints and sages, those who go against him become mean people. By paraphrasing the *Mencius*, Yan Mo establishes a link between the typical Confucian opposition of saint or sage (聖, 賢) and mean people (小 人) and the following of God. They serve as an introduction to section 2b.

---

[21] Compare Gilson, ch.V; on the use of these attributes in modern theology, see Gu Hansong (Gutheinz), pp.377 ff. (with corresponding biblical references).

[22] *Tianzhu shiyi*, p.397,8 (60).

[23] Cf. *Tianzhu shiyi*, p.525,1 (328); pp.582-583 (468-469); p.588,8 (481).

[24] *Tianzhu shiyi*, pp.415-416 (104-108): *Doctrine of the Mean* 19 = [62]; *Book of Odes* ode 274,1 = [49]; ode 276,3 = [51]; ode 304,3 = [34]; ode 236,3 = [45]; Yijing = not quoted by Yan Mo; *Liji* (two citations) = not quoted by Yan Mo; *Book of Documents* Tangshi (10), pp.173-174 = [8]; Tanggao (12), p.185 = [11]; Jinteng (34) = [30]. Elsewhere in his book, Ricci has other quotations related to God from the Chinese Classics, see list in translation by Lancashire, pp.483-485.

4.1.3 God and the human being: historical argument

Section 2b fully develops the relationship between the human being and God. The historical approach which is employed in this section is essential to understand its originality. As stated in the conclusion to this section, it is precisely because so many saints and sages served the High Lord that the ancient expression of *Shangdi* is equal to *Tianzhu*. This is an argument in which historical experience adds a special dimension. It is written by a Chinese who has an emotional bond with these saints and sages of the past. Special reference is made to Yao, Shun, Yu, Tang, the Duke of Zhou, Confucius and Mencius. A person belonging to a different culture lacks this emotional bond.

The key word in this section is the appointment by Heaven (*ming*). This refers to the Mandate given by Heaven to the ancient sovereigns to support their reign. Yan Mo also uses the term in this sense. Many of his examples refer to a political context (transmission of the throne, appointing officers, performing punishing expeditions, establishing the country and the capital). He underlines the role of the sovereign in performing the work of Heaven. But Yan certainly gives the term a larger meaning than that. Saints and sages are not only kings and sovereigns. All people are called to follow the appointment given to them by Heaven in all their "walkings and doings". Virtuous life is based on human reverence (敬) and service (事) of Heaven.

4.1.4. Without beginning, Trinity, Creation: textual approach

The third section is apologetic in nature. Three questions are discussed: 1) God being without a beginning; 2) the Trinity; 3) creation. None of them are said to appear in ancient Chinese books. Although this objection was raised by Western opponents, who take the absence as an argument "not to consider the High Lord as the Master of Heaven", it was also a very common objection of Chinese opponents of Christianity. The fact that the author refers to the difficulty to understand these mysteries, especially the Trinity, seems to indicate that here he addresses himself in the first place to the objection of a Chinese (missionaries were supposed to know what the Trinity was). The stress on the difficulty to understand it is not as such abnormal. This argument can be found in many writings, also those of missionaries. It corresponds to Thomas' opinion that the Trinity depends in no way upon philosophical knowledge. Although man is not forbidden to apply his mind to this mystery, he cannot pretend, without destroying it as a mystery, to demonstrate it by means of reason. The Trinity is known by revelation alone and therefore it eludes the grasp of human understanding.[25]

---

[25] Cf. Gilson, p.96.

The textual approach is essential for the understanding of specificity of this section. The three problems are in fact not discussed as such. One can assume that Yan Mo accepts that God is without beginning, Trinitarian and creator. Here he only investigates the absence of these notions in the Chinese scriptures. Nearly all arguments are textual: Western people only talked about these mysteries because they had access to the ancient scriptures ("canonical writings"; *gujing* 古 經). The question of God being "without beginning" and the creation are partially solved by reference to two other attributes of God ("intelligent and powerful" and "giving birth to the human being and its nature") for which, as shown in section 2a, corresponding citations were found in the Chinese Classics. As for the Trinity, Yan Mo states that Chinese authors were prudent in their writings. Fortunately their writings did not contain misleading expressions which could have been used as argument against the identification of *Shangdi* with *Tianzhu*. Finally, clear references to God being without beginning, creation and the Trinity can be found in Chinese writings, such as the *Zhuangzi*, the *Daodejing*[26] and the *Shiji* and *Hanshu*, but they are not appropriate enough to be quoted because they contain "too many expressions that are not pure enough".

This section underlines the importance Yan Mo pays to a text as such. The correspondence of the term *Shangdi* and *Tianzhu* is argued on the basis of the presence of the corresponding notions in ancient Chinese writings. These writings have to be reliable. He also shows an openness to another set of canonical writings that are not Chinese. Moreover, Yan Mo does not avoid answering questions of uncertainty. While acknowledging some apparent deficiencies and lacunae, he uses a common commentarial strategy to search for a way to defend the comprehensiveness of the Confucian Classics[27]. He uses quotations from the Classics to prove that Confucius did not express himself extensively on certain subjects. For Yan this absence does not make it impossible for a Chinese to believe in a Trinitarian God, who without beginning is creator of all things.

4.1.5. Heaven and Master of Heaven: literary approach

In the first part of the fourth section, Yan Mo treats the question of the use of the name "Heaven" in addition to "High Lord". Here the arguments are predominantly literary. Heaven is called a "borrowed" (借) appellation[28], what we would probably call today "analogy".

---

[26] Yan Mo does not call these works Taoist. Yet in the *Cunpupian* p.3a, he rejects the terms 玄 天 上 帝 ("The Lord of the Black [Pavilions] of Heaven": cf. Werner, p.177) and 玉 皇 大 (=上) 帝 ("Pure August Emperor on High": cf. Werner, p.598) as used in Taoism. In Yan Mo's eyes, these terms "are used by the devil in order to mislead the people". The terms were also rejected by Ricci, *Tianzhu shiyi*, p.415,1 (103).

[27] Cf. Henderson, p.140.

[28] This term also appears in a passage of the *Shishu biancuojie* (as quoted in Hou Wailu, p.1216) and of the *Zhouyi zhiyi* (Hou Wailu, p.1220).

Yan Mo is right in pointing out that "Heaven" or "sky" as such reveals greatness: "Among what human eyes can see, only Heaven is the greatest". This corresponds to modern studies of the phenomenon of religion in different cultures which have pointed out that even before any religious values have been set upon the "sky", it reveals its transcendence. The sky "symbolizes" transcendence, power and changelessness simply by being there. It exists because it is high, infinite, immovable, powerful.[29] In Yan Mo's eyes, the concept of Heaven is added to the one of "High Lord" to express the greatness of God. But it is also used separately as analogy. The examples of the District Magistrate being called "District" or the Emperor being called "Court" are well chosen[30], even though Yan Mo is not the first to use them. One finds similar arguments, in a slightly different context, in the *Tianzhu shiyi*.[31] One also finds Yan Mo's examples in Kangxi's edict of 1 December 1700, but it is difficult to establish a direct link between them.[32]

The second part of section 4, Yan Mo takes up the equation between the appellations "High Lord" and "Master of Heaven". Here a few other interesting literary arguments are added. In the same way as we use different names for the sovereign or for father, we also attribute different names to God. Nevertheless, this multiplicity of names designates a simple object, because we attribute all of them to the same object by way of judgment.[33] Still, Yan Mo is of the opinion that the term *Shangdi* is better than *Tianzhu*. The Western expression is in fact an abbreviated term, which needs further explanation to be properly understood. In this context, the reference to the term *Tianzhu* as it appears in the *Shiji* and *Hanshu* is worth noting. It puts the "Master of Heaven" on an equal footing with the "Master of Earth", the "Master of the Sun" etc. This might be one of the reasons why one rarely finds a reference to this sentence of the *Hanshu* in 17th century Chinese Christian writings.

In the final part of section 4, Yan Mo concludes his argument. Here the discussion is directly related to the coming of missionaries. These are divided into the first generation and those who newly arrived. Both groups are contrasted by those having studied ancient writings in collaboration with Chinese and those not having done any investigation, which again underscores the importance Yan pays to the study of texts. In final analysis, Yan Mo also refers to the interpretation of the Classical writings by Confucian scholars from the past. He takes a distance from the "wrong interpretation of Later Confucians" who "did not sufficiently catch the original meaning". They also made errors in their interpretation.

---

[29] Eliade, p.39.
[30] Also in *Cunpupian*, p.2b (朝廷, 殿階)
[31] Cf. *Tianzhu shiyi*, pp.418-419 (113-114): Ricci argues that when people serve Heaven, they do not serve the physical sky but God.
[32] Cf. Colombel. p.529 (朝廷, 階下).
[33] Cf. Gilson, p.108.

This is the general idea of God as presented by Yan Mo in his *Personal Discussion* by way of positive argumentation. Yet, the *Personal Discussion* is preceded by a *List of Quotations*, which does not seem to present a specific idea of God. Indeed, the comments added to these quotations are rather factual. Still, any selection of quotations contains an interpretation in itself. The changes that Yan Mo brought into these quotations can also tell us something about his idea of God.

4.2. Difference between Yan Mo and the Song commentaries

A question to be raised here is whether there are any significant differences between Yan Mo's idea of Heaven and the interpretation by Song commentators, as he seemed to imply at the end of the *Personal Discussion*. From a comparison of the Song commentaries and the selection Yan Mo made of them, there appears a quite obvious difference in the interpretation of *tian* and *shangdi*. Generally speaking these differences concern passages where Zhu Xi, or his disciple Cai Chen, interpret *tian* in the sense of principle (*li* 理)[34].

There are three categories of passages where such differences appear: replacement, omission and alteration.

4.2.1. Replacement

A first group of passages concern the replacement of the character *tian* by *shangdi*. At several instances, in his commentary on the *Book of Documents*, Cai Chen uses the character *tian* instead of *shangdi*, although in the passage concerned the text of the *Book of Documents* uses *shangdi*. There are a few places where Yan Mo prefers to use *shangdi* instead.

> The clearest example[35] is the comment on [5]: 以 昭 受 上 帝 ，
> 天 其 申 命 用 休 (And you will brightly receive gifts from the High Lord. Will not Heaven renew its favouring appointment, and give you blessing?)[36]
> The *Shujing jizhuan* writes: 以 是 昭 受 于 天 ， 天 豈 不 重 命 而 用 休 美 乎[37]
> Version A changes this into: 以 此 明 受 於 上 帝 ， 天 豈 不 重 命 而 用 休 美 之 乎
> Version B changes again: 以 此 明 受 於 上 帝 ， 上 帝 豈 不 重 命 而 用 休 美 之 乎

This replacement confirms that Yan Mo preferred the term *shangdi* to *tian* as already appeared in section 4a of the *Personal Discussion*. It is probably due to the fact that *shangdi* has a more anthropomorphic connotation than *tian*.

---

[34] See Chan, chap.12: "Chu Hsi on *T'ien*".
[35] Other examples: the change of *shangdi* in *tian* by version B in [13]; the omission of *huangtian* by version B in [33]; in [26] both versions keep *tian* as mentioned in the *Shujing jizhuan*, while the text of the *Book of Documents* has *shangdi*.
[36] Yiji (5), p.79.
[37] *Shujing jizhuan*, p.18.

4.2.2. Omission

A second group of passages concerns the omission of some parts of the Song commentaries. As mentioned before, Yan Mo did not copy the whole of the Song commentaries (this would have enlarged his work enormously), but he made only a selection of them. In general, these selections are faithful and catch the meaning of the passages concerned well. The only exception is passages concerning *tian* and *shangdi*. Not all omissions of references to *tian* and *shangdi* are equally important, but some omissions appear to be very conscious.

a) A first example concerns the omission of Cheng Yi's 程頤 (1033-1107) well-known interpretation of *tian*, which was also adopted by Zhu Xi[38]. (the passage between brackets and in italics is the one omitted by Yan Mo)

[58] = Ode 192,4.

〔瞻彼中林，侯薪侯蒸〕民今方殆，視天夢夢，既克有定，靡人弗勝，有皇上帝，伊誰云憎。

〔興也。中林，林中也。侯，維也。薪，大者；蒸，小者。民今方危殆，而視天反夢夢然，〔上天則疾無時，亦曰此危也。〕殆，危也。〔林殆，謂中林殆。〕維皇，以形體謂之天，以主宰謂之帝。〔見于惡則憎之，於善則福之。此民天特天福，人已勝之。〕中林明。程子曰：帝可于惡則憎然，當然勝天。神、主幸，別豈上則眾勝天。夢之主號，既有上則眾〕。天其維薪，呼於分及夫二人〕帝。以維痛意爾。自⋯：〕

Look into the middle of the forest, there are only large faggots and small branches in it. The people are now in peril, they look on Heaven as undiscerning. But let its determination be fixed, and there is none whom it will not overcome. The August High Lord, whom does he hate?

---

38 See also Chan, p.184.

This is an allegory[39]. 中 林 means "in the middle of the forest"; 侯 means "only"; 殆 means "peril"; 夢 夢 means "not clear"; and 皇 means "august". 上 帝 is the positive force of Heaven. Cheng [Yi] said that in the sense of physical shape it is called tian (heaven), and in the sense of ruler di (lord).[40]

Here is said that in a forest you can easily distinguish the large faggots from the small branches. But now people are in peril and distress and they cry and appeal to Heaven, but they see Heaven as undiscerning as if it appears unable to discriminate between the good and the bad. Yet this is only for the time that it is not fixed. When it is fixed, there is nothing that is not overcome by Heaven. How would Heaven hate and punish any one? To bless the good and to punish the evil is the normal principle of High Heaven[41] [instead of: is only a natural principle]. Shen Baoxu[42] said: [The saying] "When people are numerous, they overcome Heaven; when Heaven is fixed, it can also overcome man" comes probably from this passage.

The first passage omitted by Yan Mo contains Zhu Xi's explanation of the term shangdi. Zhu Xi refers to Cheng Yi's explanation. The original passage reads:

乾 天 也 。 夫 天 專 言 之 ， 則 道 也 ， 天 且 弗 違 是
也 。 分 而 言 之 ， 則 以 形 體 謂 之 天 ， 以 主 宰 謂
之 帝 ， 以 功 用 謂 之 鬼 神 ， 以 妙 用 謂 之 神 ， 以
性 情 謂 之 乾 。 乾 者 萬 物 之 始 ， 故 爲 天 ， 爲 陽
， 爲 父 ， 爲 君 。

"Qian is Heaven (tian). Spoken of in a specific sense, tian is the Way, and Heaven does not go against the Way. Spoken of separately, it is called tian in the sense of physical shape, di (lord) in the sense of ruler, passive and positive cosmic forces (guishen) in the sense of function, spirit in the sense of its wonderful operation, and qian in the sense of nature and feeling. Qian is the beginning of all things, therefore it is tian, yang, father and sovereign.[43]

---

[39] xing 興: one of the poetical genres in the Book of Odes, different from the metaphor or bi 比.

[40] Compare with the remark made by J. Legge, p.316, n.4: "The account of those two names and given by Ch'ing E [=Cheng Yi], and accepted by Choo [=Zhu Xi] and all subsequent writers, is absurd. {...} We are as good judges of what is meant by Heaven, as a name for the Supreme Power, as Ch'ing was; and however the use of it may be explained, it certainly carries our thoughts above and beyond the visible sky."

[41] Version B omits "High Heaven".

[42] Lived in the period of Spring and Autumn, around 500 B.C.

[43] Cf. Chan, p.184: Yizhuan 易 傳 (Commentary on the Book of Changes), 1:1a, in the Er Cheng quanshu 二 程 全 書 (Complete Works of the Two Chengs).

At first sight, it might seem surprising that this explanation is rejected by Yan Mo. Cheng Yi seems to argue that these different terms all refer to one and the same subject. Moreover, in his *Personal Discussion* Yan Mo has also pointed out how a term like *Tian* can be used as analogy for *Shangdi* or *Tianzhu*. Yet Cheng Yi's explanation was also rejected earlier in Ricci's *Tianzhu shiyi*[44], which may help us to understand Yan Mo's discarding of it. Ricci basically rejects this explanation because God has "no form". He argues that one should serve God reverently and not serve the created things (such as the sky) which God has provided for our use. One can assume that Yan Mo rejected Cheng Yi's explanation, because of the possible confusion between the Creator and the created (which also include *guishen* "devils and angels").

It is also worth noting that the final sentence of Zhu Xi's comment was not retained. It presents the idea of a Heaven very much subjected to the will of the people.

b) A second example of omission is the very conscious refusal to interpret *tian* as principle.

[60]= *Analects* III,13

獲 罪 於 天 ， 無 所 禱 也 。

天 〔 即 理 也 。 其 〕 尊 無 對 。 〔 非 奧 灶 之 可 比
也 。 〕 逆 理 〔 則 〕 獲 罪 於 天 〔 矣 〕 。 豈 〔 媚
於 奧 灶 = 〕 他 禱 所 能 〔 禱 而 〕 免 乎 ？ 〔 言 但
當 順 理 非 特 不 當 媚 灶 亦 不 可 媚 於 奧 也 。 〕

He who offends against Heaven has none to whom he can pray.

Heaven means principle.[45] *It has no equal in respect. [The gods of] the furnace and [of] the south-west corner cannot be compared with it. If* one goes against the principle[46], *then* (=and) one offends against Heaven. How could one be acquitted by praying to another (=*flattering [the gods of] the furnace and [of] the south-west corner? Here is only said that one should follow the principle, it is not so that one is not allowed to flatter [the god of] the furnace or [of] the south-west corner.*

---

[44] *Tianzhu shiyi*, p.417,1-2 (109).
[45] Compare with the remark made by Legge, p.159 n.13: "Chu Hsi says "Heaven means principle". But why should Heaven mean principle, if there were not in such a use of the term an instinctive recognition of a supreme government of intelligence and righteousness?"
[46] Version B also omits this part (逆 理).

This comment of Zhu Xi is one of the key-passages for his understanding of *tian*. As W.T. Chan has pointed out, it is to be expected that Zhu Xi interpret *tian* in the sense of principle.[47] This idea is also derived from Cheng Yi, but Zhu Xi refined it and gave it a new meaning. Traditionally, to offend against, obey, violate, delight in, or stand in awe of Heaven had been understood in terms of Heaven being an anthropomorphic deity or at least a cosmic power. To interpret Heaven in the sense of principle was a new proposition, and a daring one at that. Moreover, as illustrated by this passage, Zhu Xi explicitly identified *tian* with principle, thus carrying Cheng Yi's interpretation a step further. Once more, Yan Mo gives no explanation why he has left out this passage. But one can again assume that he basically agreed with the Jesuit position which opposed the identification of God with *li*, because God was said to be at the origin of *li* and *qi* 氣 (matter-energy).[48]

c) There are also examples of omission where the interpretation of *tianming* or *ming* as *li* is rejected.

> In the commentary on [15] the following passage of the *Shujing jizhuan*[49] is omitted: 明 命 者 ， 上 天 顯 然 之 理 ， 而 命 之 我 者 。 在 天 爲 明 命 ， 在 人 爲 明 德 (The clear mandate is the apparent principle of High Heaven which is mandated to us. In Heaven it is called "clear mandate" and among men it is called "clear virtue").

> In the commentary on [61], Yan Mo discards the following passage of the *Sishu jizhu*[50]: 天 命 者 天 所 賦 之 正 理 也 (The Mandate of Heaven is the correct principle conferred by Heaven).

These passages are clear reflections of Zhu Xi's thought, for whom, in the final analysis, Heaven is identical with *ming*, and *ming* is the function of principle. When a pupil inquired whether it is not true that Heaven is spoken of from the point of view of what is natural; *ming* (mandate, destiny) from the point of view of its operation and its endowment in things and principle from the point of view of everything having a specific principle (*ze* 則) of its being, Zhu Xi gave an affirmative answer. He also said, "Principle is the substance of Heaven, *ming* is the function of principle...". Heaven and *ming* are not two different things.[51] In Yan Mo's eyes, however, God and *ming* are two different things, because *ming* cannot simply be considered as a function of principle. *Ming* is rather like an order, a mandate that was given to the

---

[47] Chan, pp.185-186.
[48] This matter is discussed in the *Tianzhu shiyi*, p.406 ff. (84)
[49] *Shujing jizhuan*, p.49.
[50] *Analects* XVI,8.
[51] Chan, pp.186-187; quotations from *Zhuzi yulei* 朱 子 語 類 V,1 and 2.

sages but is given to every person as well, so as to serve God and to be reverent to God.

The fact that these three types of omissions are all conscious omissions can be confirmed by the following explicit rejection in Yan Mo's *Shishu biancuojie*:

"Zhu Xi said that Heaven is principle... and that the Mandate of Heaven is the correct principle conferred by Heaven. ... But he did not recognize that there is one High Lord who is supreme powerful, and supreme purely spiritual, and that he created heaven, earth, and all things and that he supervises them. The physical heaven is only one of the things he created, it is not the High Lord himself. Moreover, {Zhu Xi] did not realize that ancient people used this character *tian* as a borrowed appellation, as a result of which he misunderstood Heaven as having the two aspects of principle (*li*) and matter-energy (*qi*): sometimes it is specifically talked about in the sense of form, sometimes in terms of principle. Moreover he said that the blue-sky heaven is precisely this heaven of the way and principle. He was completely wrong in his deliberation."[52]

What was implicitly indicated through the omissions in the previous quotations, is explicitly said in this text. Heaven as cosmic principle and energy contradicts Yan Mo's vision of a God who is powerful and spiritual, who is a creator and a ruler. Once more, his opinion and arguments might not be very original, but it is important that they are said by a person belonging to Chinese culture.

Yet, the rejection of the interpretation of *tian* or *tianming* in the sense of principle, does not mean the complete rejection of the concept "principle" (*li*) by Yan Mo. This term appears, for instance, in the explanation of 義 as 理 之 當 然 (necessity of the principle) in [20] or of 彝 倫 as 常 理 (constant principles) in [29]. Moreover, in [40] there is an interesting example where Yan Mo follows the *Shijing jizhuan*[53] interpretation of 順 帝 之 則 (to follow the pattern of the Lord) as 循 天 理 (to follow the Heavenly principles).

---

[52] Section of *Shishu biancuojie* as quoted in Hou Wailu, p.1216; compare also with *Cunpupian*, p.2b.
[53] *Shijing jizhu*, p.126.

4.2.3. Alteration

A third group of passages are those where the meaning is clearly altered. The different changes to an excerpt of the comment to [25] are a good example.

> The original text of the *Shujing*[54] writes: 民 之 所 欲 ， 天 必 從 之 (What the people desire, Heaven will necessarily follow).
> The *Shujing jizhuan*[55] remains close to this text: 民 有 所 欲 ， 天 必 從 之 (When the people have desires, Heaven necessarily will follow them).
> Version A has changed it into: 民 有 所 欲 ， 天 無 不 從 之 (When the people have desires, Heaven will (not not) follow them)
> Version B has changed it again: 天 ... 從 民 所 欲 (Heaven ... follows what the people desire).

From these different versions it appears that the author was struggling with the "necessity" by which Heaven would be bound to follow the people's desires, and that he sought a way to avoid such an interpretation.

Another example of alteration is the attenuation of the radical tone of an interpretation.

> The text of the *Shijing*[56] in [53] reads 上 帝 板 板 ， 下 民 卒 癉 (The High Lord has become stern and the lower people are full of distress).
> The *Shijing jizhuan*[57] gives the following interpretation: 天 反 其 常 道 而 使 民 盡 病 矣 (Heaven has reversed its constant way and has caused the people to be full of distress).
> Yan Mo, gives a more euphemistic interpretation: 天 欲 安 民 而 今 反 其 常 ， 是 必 有 所 致 之 者 (Heaven wants to give peace to the people, but has now reversed its constancy; there certainly must be a reason that caused it).

The reasons for these changes are different from the previous omissions. Here the motive is predominantly theological in nature. The texts are altered so as to portray a God that is less fierce and less subject to the will of the people.

---

[54] Taishi (*shang*) (27), p.288.
[55] *Shujing jizhuan*, p.67.
[56] Ode 254,1.
[57] *Shijing jizhuan*, p.136.

4.3. Concluding remarks

In our analysis we have seen how Yan Mo paid a special attention to the "text" as such in order to sustain his argument. He has done this in a very systematic and orderly way. Moreover, the large number of quotations from other texts makes his own text very dense.

In fact we face different types of texts. Firstly there are the original writings or Classics (*Book of Documents*, *Book of Odes*, *Analects*, *Doctrine of the Mean*, *Mencius*). Secondly there are the comments on these texts (mainly by Cai Chen and Zhu Xi). Finally there is Yan Mo's own text. In addition, one should also mention that Yan Mo makes reference to the Western Classical writings. All these join together in the *Ditiankao*. Yan Mo was fortunate to have a readership (the Western missionaries) who were interested in textual arguments. Therefore, Yan Mo's writing can be considered as a dialogue between two traditions, Chinese and Western, in which texts were highly valued as such.

One of the characteristics of Yan Mo's text is that it proceeds by quotation. Every quotation establishes a relation or better a dialogue between two texts, between the original text and the text in which this original text is quoted[58]. However, it is not a simple relationship. It goes further. A quotation establishes a dialogue between two systems, each of them composed of a text and a subject. A new significance arises out of this interaction. It is usually the new context that gives a new interpretation to the quotation. This is obvious in Yan Mo's text. He has given a new interpretation to the Chinese Classical texts both by the way of explicit quotation and omission (like in the case of the Song commentaries).

Yan Mo rejects most of the Neo-Confucian interpretation and goes back to the "unpolished" meaning. He discovers in the Classical texts the attributes of God presented in Thomistic theology. Moreover, he brings these quotations into the context of his belief in a Trinitarian God, without beginning, but creator of all things. On the whole, these characteristics present God in a descriptive and rational way.

Like any dialogue, however, the dialogue established by a quotation is not one-way street. A quotation is not only affected by the new context. It also affects the horizon of the text in which it is quoted. It is not just that *shangdi* and *tian* are interpreted as being similar to the Christian *tianzhu*; God is also given particularities which belong to his name as *shangdi* and *tian*: Chinese terms for human values like *ren* 仁 and *yi* 義 are attributed to God in perfection; the following of God is linked with the Confucian opposition of "saints" (*shengren*) and "mean people" (*xiaoren*); but most important, God is related to the history of Chinese saints and sages who have

---

[58] For a theory of "quotation" see Compagnon, esp. p.34 ff., p.56.

served him and obeyed his mandate throughout the ages. Here, the historical narrative element is predominant.

Yan Mo was not the only one who looked at the Classics with new insight or who dared to differ from the orthodox interpretation of the Song commentators. Many of his contemporaries did so, the most famous example being Yan Ruoju 閻若璩 (1636-1704).[59] Yet, he is rather unique in bringing these texts into dialogue with another system of thought and practice, the Christian faith.

In order to appreciate even more the extent to which he gave a new interpretation or not, we proceed now to the second part of this dissertation. For a while, we leave aside Yan Mo's text. We will look directly at the Classics. Then, at the end of this investigation, we will take up Yan Mo's text again.

---

[59] On this topic see Elman's *From Philosophy to Philology*.

PART II:

ON THE IDEA OF THE DEITIES "HEAVEN" OR "LORD" IN THE *BOOK OF DOCUMENTS*, THE *BOOK OF ODES*, THE *ANALECTS* AND THE *MENCIUS*

Chapter 5: Methodology

In the second part of this dissertation we will attempt to analyse the deities *tian* and *shangdi* as they appear in the *Book of Documents*, the *Book of Odes*, the *Analects* and the *Mencius*. Because of the special nature of the text history of these books, some preliminary methodological remarks are necessary.

5.1. The question of the texts

A first point is the background of this research. Our main research focuses on the interpretation of these works by an Early Qing Chinese Christian author. In the *Ditiankao*, Yan Mo quotes mainly the *Book of Documents*, the *Book of Odes*, the *Analects* and the *Mencius* to prove that the concepts of *tian* and *shangdi* are equivalent to the Christian God. Therefore, as a preliminary study, we wanted to know more about the concepts of *tian* and *shangdi* in these Classical writings, and much of the research was indeed done before the analysis of Yan's text.

This background has an important influence on the direction of the research in this chapter. Indeed, our research does not focus on the role of *tian* and *shangdi* in the Zhou ideology. Such an historical approach is, of course, fully acceptable. Herrlee Creel did pioneer research in this field.[1] The early analysis by Tien Tchéu-kang still remains a stimulating reference.[2] The

---

[1] Creel's "Appendix C: The Origin of the Deity T'ien" is based on an article originally published in Chinese in 1935.
[2] Tien studied the idea of God in eight Chinese Classics but also incorporated the results of archeological discoveries.

writings of Fu Pei-jung[3] and Robert Eno[4] include the latest research on both concepts in the Zhou dynasty. Due to their approach, these authors first take into account the historicity of the texts they use, distinguishing the different levels of redaction that exist in each of the early writings. As we have seen in the previous chapter, a scholar like Yan Mo was to a certain extent also aware of the different redactions that most of these writings underwent, especially in the Eastern Han dynasty. Still, like many of his contemporaries, he also used these texts *as a whole*. Therefore, in this chapter we will take the four texts *as a whole* as well.

Let us illustrate this approach by taking the *Book of Documents*, the most corrupt texts of the four, as an example. In much of their research, Fu Pei-jung and Robert Eno are interested in the role of *tian* and *shangdi* in the Western Zhou ideology. Most of their arguments, therefore, are based on documents gathered from the oracle-bone inscriptions and bronze-inscriptions, supplemented by sections from the *Book of Odes*, but the *Book of Documents* takes only a limited place in their research. This is due to the historical status of the text, and more precisely to the difference between the New and Old Text version.[5]

Fu Pei-jung bases himself mainly on the twelve sections that are said to represent the ideas of the early Western Zhou.[6] Eno's scepticism extends to these twelve sections accepted as "genuine" by several authors.[7] We share much of the scepticism of these authors and agree that it is difficult to rely on the *Book of Documents* for evidence for early Zhou thought and practices.

We will, nevertheless, attempt to study the idea of Heaven in the *Book of Documents as a whole*. By doing this, we do not deny the differences between the New and Old Text versions.[8] But it is one thing to make an historical study of the idea of Heaven in let us say the Shang and Zhou dynasties, but another to study the effect that a given text has produced through history (*Wirkungsgeschichte*)[9]. For this purpose, one has to take the

---

[3] Fu Pei-jung obtained his Ph.D. degree at Yale Univ. in 1984 with a dissertation on "The Concept if *T'ien* in Ancient China: With Special Emphasis on Confucianism"; it was published in Chinese in 1985.

[4] Robert Eno obtained his Ph.D. degree at the Univ. of Michigan in 1984 with a dissertation on "The Role of *T'ien* in the Teachings of the Early Juist Community"; it was published in 1990 (1990a). In addition on can also refer to an article on "The Notions of God in the Ancient Chinese Religion" by J. Shih (1969).

[5] For a good summary of the date and authenticity of the *Book of Documents*, see Loewe, pp.376 ff.

[6] Fu (1984), p.26-27; in fact, at several instances, he also quotes from Old Text sections.

[7] Eno (1990a), p.210 n.12; Eno (1984), pp.122-124.

[8] We will keep the difference by underlining the corresponding number of the Old Text chapters. Moreover, all major conclusions of this paper have a serious foundation in New Text version chapters; Old Text versions reinforce the argument.

[9] Term created by Gadamer (p.267 ff.) but now commonly used in exegesis.

text as a whole. In other words, the Tang, Song and Ming authors who read the *Book of Documents* were influenced by the whole of the text. They had no bone-inscriptions at hand and hardly distinguished between the "genuine" and "falsified" version of the *Book of Documents*. To a certain extent, this was also true for the early-Confucians (or Ruists). The idea they formulated of Heaven had one of the circulating versions of the *Book of Documents* and *Book of Odes* as a background. Looking at the quotations from the *Book of Documents* and *Book of Odes* in their writings, they took them as a genuine reflection of Zhou dynasty thought and practices.

To summarize the aim of the second part of this book: our focus is not the question "What was the primordial notion of Heaven in China?" but "What is the notion of Heaven in the *Book of Documents, Book of Odes*, the *Analects* and the *Mencius*?" (since it is this notion that had a major effect on later tradition). We have limited ourselves to these four texts since they were most influential to Yan Mo. The *Great Learning* and *Doctrine of the Mean* could have been added as well. They were not included because they had only a minor presence in Yan Mo's *Ditiankao* (no quotation from the *Great Learning* and only one from the *Doctrine of the Mean*). Comparisons with the *Xunzi* and the *Mozi* would be worthwhile, but would request a separate study.

5.2. Heaven and the human being

A second methodological question is how to study the idea of Heaven. For instance, can the author as a foreigner enter into the world of the *Book of Documents* and have some proper understanding of the idea of Heaven, without projecting his Western-Christian ideas on the Chinese Heaven? Here, we basically face the same problem as a 20th Century Chinese who is reading these texts (or simply any person reading a text): while being aware of one's proper subjectivity and danger of "in-egesis", one should still look for ways to discover what the text wants to say and search for a proper "fusion of the horizons" (*Horizontverschmelzung*)[10].

More important is the question which way of analysis should be adopted. The choice for a traditional Chinese way of analysis is not impossible. One can refer to Cheng Yi's analysis which was also adopted by Zhu Xi. As mentioned before, Cheng Yi approached Heaven from the point of view of concepts like "physical shape", "ruler", "function" etc. On the basis of this terminology, one could similarly try to find in which case a specific term is used in the sense of physical shape, of ruler, of function etc. Yet, the greatest limit of this approach is that it is closely connected with Song-Ming Neo-Confucianism, and not necessarily more suitable for today. Moreover, much of it was explicitly rejected by Yan Mo.

---

[10] Term used in Gadamer's hermeneutic method (p.273 ff).

Research on the notion of Heaven has chosen different ways. Feng Youlan defined a fivefold meaning for Heaven: a material or physical *Tian*, a ruling or presiding *Tian*, a fatalistic *Tian*, a naturalistic *Tian* and an ethical *Tian*.[11] Tien Tchéu-kang used a scholastic approach, searching for the different attributes of Heaven (omnipresence, intelligence, uniqueness, almighty, etc.).[12] More recently, Fu Pei-jung, classifies the characters used for Heaven under the notions of "Dominator" (統 治 者), "Creator" (造 生 者), "Sustainer" (載 行 者), "Revealer" (啓 示 者), and "Judge" (審 判 者).[13] Eno, on his side, analyses *tian* in terms of the "prescriptive" and "descriptive" aspects.[14] The use of these notions certainly throws new light on certain concepts of Heaven as they appear in the Classics. Moreover it also has the advantage of a more systematic approach, in line with contemporary philosophy of religion and philosophy of language. It is not our intention to repeat simply what they have said and we do not intend to summarize their analysis. We will only try to look at the same texts from a different perspective.

The approach we would like to adopt is the following: the starting point will be the relationship between Heaven and the human being: 天 人 (which as such is not very original). We would like to understand the notion of Heaven, through its relationship with the human being. The questions that will be raised in this context are: "Who is in contact with Heaven?", "What type of relationship is it?" For example, in the analysis of the famous sentence "The Master said: ...At fifty, I knew the Decree of Heaven" (子 曰 ： 五 十 而 知 天 命)[15], our first question will not be "Is this an immanent, transcendent or personal God?" or "What is meant by Decree?" but rather: "Who says this sentence and what is his relationship with Heaven?" In the conclusion we will refer to similar analyses in other cultures, using, by way of comparison, more universal theories of religion proposed by Rudolf Otto and Mircea Eliade. Throughout the analysis of the four texts, we will try to follow the same approach and limit ourselves to the above questions. The analysis of the *Book of Documents* will be the longest, not only because of the extent of the work itself, but also because some fundamental elements that are proposed in this text, are repeated in one or another way in the other writings.

---

[11] Fung (1931), vol.I, p.31; cf. Fu (1984), (abstract p.i); Eno (1990a), p.4; see also rejection of this approach by Fu (1993), p.310.

[12] Cf. Tien, third part (p.129 ff.).

[13] Fu (1984), p.28; Fu presented an extensive explanation of the use of the five notions in Fu (1993) (originally published in 1986); it is important to underline that the concepts used by Fu have the Chinese terms at their origin.

[14] Eno (1990a), pp.82, 102. Prescriptively, *Tian* provides reasons to act in certain ways in the future: we should do *X* because *Tian* wants us to and/or will reward on: *Tian* serves as a normative value standard. Descriptively, *Tian* provides a reason why events in the past occurred as they did: *Tian* wished it so.

[15] *Analects* II,4.

Chapter 6: The *Book of Documents*

6.1. Statistical analysis

As a first step of our analysis we will include a statistical analysis. Such an analysis has only a limited value. It is insufficient, but it is a necessary step which can also throw some light on the use of the terms in the given texts. Moreover, as seen in the previous chapter, Yan Mo himself was interested by the different terms that were used.

After having identified all passages related to the deities "Heaven" and "Lord" in the *Book of Documents*, the enclosed table was established.

One can differentiate between twelve different character combinations with regard to the notion of "Heaven" and "Lord":[1]

---

[1] Note on the selection procedure: all the *tian* characters have been selected, even if in some cases it is not absolutely certain whether a deity is meant (see e.g. Yaodian (1), p.24: 滔 天 (twice) (cf. Tien, p.28); see the same combination also in Yiji (5), p.77; another example is the combination 天 邑 商 (Duoshi (42), p.460) where it probably means "great" (cf. Creel, p.498); under *tianming* have also been included: 天 之 命 in Yiji (5) (once) and in Duofang (46) (four times), 天 明 命 in Xianyouyide (17) (once); 天 之 明 命 in Taijia (*shang*) (14), 天 永 命 in Shaogao (40) (three times); the longer combination of *tian* with *ming* has been classified under *tian* (cf. in Luogao (41), p.436: 王 如 弗 敢 及 天 基 命 定命); the combination *tianxia* ("all under heaven" or "empire") has been included for reference (in Yiji (5) also once 天 之 下), even if it seems that it no longer included the notion of a deity; under *di* have been excluded the cases where *di* refers to the sovereign (cf. Tien, p.76); under (*shang)diming* have been included 帝 之 命 in Duofang (46) and 上 帝 之 耿 命 in Lizheng (47).
On the different names see also Tien, p.45 seq.
In this dissertation the page numbers refer the Legge edition of the *Book of Documents*, but the translation is not necessarily his (compared often with Kalgren's translation).

tian (天): 184
shangtian (上 天): 4
huangtian (皇 天): 14
haotian (昊 天): 1
mintian (旻 天): 2
tianming (天 命): 37
tiandao (天 道): 5
tianzi (天 子): 8
tianxia (天 下): 18

di (帝): 16
shangdi (上 帝): 26
huangshangdi (皇 上 帝): 1
huangtianshangdi (皇 天 上 帝): 1
(shang)diming (上 帝 命): 5

Here a short note on the translation of these terms is appropriate. As already done in the previous chapter, the character *tian* 天 will be further translated "Heaven", although its original meaning might be a variant of *da* 大 , meaning "great" or "large".[2] The character *di* 帝 will be translated "Lord", and *shangdi* 上 帝 as "High Lord".[3] One could also translate it "God", if one wants to stress its being a deity.[4] While there are divergent theories on the origin of the character and notion *di* 帝,[5] there is more agreement on the

---

[2] On the origin of *Tian*, see Creel; for a discussion of Creel's theory see also Appendix A "The Origins of the Term '*T'ien*'" in Eno (1990a), pp.181-189; *tian* could also be translated as "sky".

[3] *Di* could also be translated "Sovereign", *shangdi* "Lord-on-high" or "Sovereign-on-high"; while *shang* can also mean "on-high", it seems more obvious to consider is as simply "high" such as in the combination *shangtian* "High Heaven"; this translation is also adopted by Allan.

[4] Kalgren uses the term "God"; compare for an interesting discussion on the translations of these terms by Legge, a reflection twenty years after his first translation of the *Book of Documents*: Legge (1879), pp.xxii-xxix.

[5] For the most recent discussion, see Eno (1990b) who calls into question a consensus belief that the term *di* (and the term *shangdi*), as used in the Shang oracle texts, denoted a supreme deity. No matter what the exact origin of either *di* or *tian*, one can agree with Eno that as far as the their use in the *Book of Documents* is concerned, these are "retrospective reconstructions" (p.15) which tell us more about the Chou and later periods than about the origin of these terms.

Terms in the *Book of Documents*

		帝	上帝	皇上帝	皇天上帝	上帝命	天	上天	皇天	昊天	旻天	天命	天道	天子	天下
1	Yaodian 堯典						2								
2	Shundian 舜典		1				1			1					1
3	Dayumo 大禹謨						5						1		3
4	Gaoyaomo 皋陶謨						6					1			
5	Yiji 益稷		1				2					1			1
6	Yugong 禹貢														
7	Ganshi 甘誓						2		1						
8	Wuzizhige 五子之歌														1
9	Yinzheng 胤征						5							1	
10	Tangshi 湯誓		1				1					1			
11	Zhonghuizhigao 仲虺之誥	1					3	1				2	1		
12	Tanggao 湯誥		1	1			1	2	1			2	1		
13	Yixun 伊訓		1				1		1						
14	Taijia (shang) 太甲上						1					1			
15	Taijia (zhong) 太甲中						1		1						
16	Taijia (xia) 太甲下		1				2					1			
17	Xianyouyide 咸有一德						5		1			1			
18	Pangeng (shang) 盤庚上						2					1			

#		帝	上帝	皇上帝	皇天上帝	上帝命	天	上天	皇天	昊天	旻天	天命	天道	天子	天下
19	Pangeng (*zhong*) 盤庚中						2								
20	Pangeng (*xia*) 盤庚下		1												
21	Shuoming (*shang*) 說命上	1												1	1
22	Shuoming (*zhong*) 說命中						1						1		
23	Shuoming (*xia*) 說命下													1	1
24	Gaozongrongyi 高宗肜日						4		1					1	
25	Xibokanli 西伯戡黎						6								
26	Weizi 微子						1							1	
27	Taishi (*shang*) 泰誓上		3				7	1	1			1			
28	Taishi (*zhong*) 泰誓中						8					1			
29	Taishi (*xia*) 泰誓下		1				3								
30	Mushi 牧誓						1								
31	Wucheng 武成		1				4		1			1			4
32	Hongfan 洪範	2	2				2							2	1
33	Lüao 旅獒	1													
34	Jinteng 金縢						5								
35	Dagao 大誥		2				15					3			

88

		帝	上帝	皇上帝	皇天上帝	上帝命	天	上天	皇天	昊天	旻天	天命	天道	天子	天下
37	Kanggao 康誥	1	1									1			
38	Jiugao 酒誥						7								
39	Zicai 梓材						7		1						
40	Shaogao 召誥		1		1		10		1			6			1
41	Luogao 洛誥						3					1			
42	Duoshi 多士	7	2				14					2			
43	Wuyi 無逸						1					1			
44	Junshi 君奭		3			1	15		1			1			
45	Caizhongzhiming 蔡仲之命								1						
46	Duofang 多方	2				1	14					7			
47	Lizheng 立政	1	2			1								1	1
48	Zhouguan 周官						1								
49	Junchen 君陳														
50	Guming 顧命		1				4								1
51	Kangwangzhigao 康王之誥								2					1	1
52	Biming 畢命												1		1

		帝	上帝	皇上帝	皇天上帝	上帝命	天	上天	皇天	昊天	旻天	天命	天道	天子	天下
53	Junya 君牙														
54	Jiongming 冏命														
55	Lüxing 呂刑		2				8					1			1
56	Wenhouzhiming 文侯之命		1				1								
57	Bishi 費誓														
58	Qinshi 秦誓														
	Total	16	26	1	1	5	184	4	14	1	2	37	5	8	18

The chapters of which the numbers are underlined are Old Text chapters.

evolution it underwent.[6] Lord was considered as the (highest) deity by the Shang people. But when the Shang kings arrogated the title *di* to honour their ancestors, and also called them "lord" (a notion that often appears in the *Book of Documents*), the supremacy of the Lord had to be affirmed, and he was called "High Lord".

From this "statistical" approach a few conclusions can be drawn. Relatively few chapters (less than one fifth of all the chapters) make no mention of the deities Heaven or Lord. These are: Yugong (6), Lüao (33), Junchen (49), Junya (53), Jiongming (54), Bishi (57), Qinshi (58) (the numbers refer to the chapter number of the enclosed list, the underlined numbers are Old text chapters)[7]. On the other hand there are a few dense theologal texts: Dagao (35), Shaogao (40), Duoshi (42), Junshi (44), Duofang (46) (except for no.40, the texts are related to the Duke of Zhou[8]).

The dominant concept is that of *tian*, the deity of the Zhou, which in history gradually replaced the concept of *di*, the (highest) deity of the Shang. Most analysts consider that in the *Book of Documents* both notions are to be considered as interchangeable.[9] In several passages this equation is even very obvious.[10] Moreover, there seems to be an interplay between the two concepts,[11] (as was also pointed out by Yan Mo).

Worth noting also are the prefixes added to *tian* or *di*. Historically, the priority of *di* was affirmed by its becoming *shangdi*. While the term *tian* is most often used separately, one also finds three references to *shangtian*. It is not impossible that this occurred under the influence of the term *shangdi*.

---

[6] Fu (1984), pp.1-22, esp. p.16-17; for an overview of the different theories on the evolution of *shangdi* to *tian* by mainland scholars see Ren Jiyu, chap, 2 and 3 and especially pp.79-82 and also Feng Youlan (1982), pp.60-70.

[7] In Zhouguan (48) it is not certain whether *tian* has a theologal meaning; in Wuzizhige (8) the only appearance of *tian* is in the combination *tianxia*.

[8] On the role of the Duke of Zhou, see Feng Youlan (1982), pp.66-67.

[9] Cf. Fu (1984), pp.28 ff. and Eno (1990b), pp.14-15; from a linguistic and philosophical point of view, Tien correctly states: "Di se rapporte à Dieu par définition et Tian par métaphore ou image, c'est-à-dire: Dieu gouverne le monde entier comme le ciel couvre tous les êtres dans son immensité infinie" (p.46).

[10] E.g. Tangshi (10), pp.173-174: 有 夏 多 罪 ， 天 命 殛 之 。 。 。 夏 氏 有 罪 ， 予 畏 上 帝 ， 不 敢 不 正 。

Zhonghuizhigao (11), p.179: ...茲 率 厥 典 ， 奉 若 天 命 。 夏 王 有 罪 ， 矯 誣 上 天 ， 以 布 命 于 下 ， 帝 用 不 臧 ...

Taishi (*xia*) (29), pp.295-296: 上 帝 弗 順 ， 祝 降 時 喪 。 爾 其 孜 孜 奉 予 一 人 ， 恭 行 天 罰 。

Duofang (46), p.492: 洪 惟 圖 天 之 命 ... and p.496: 厥 圖 帝 之 命 。

[11] Duoshi (42), p.454-457: 天 ， 昊 天 ， 天 命 ， 帝 ， 上 帝 (天 不 畀 。 。 。 帝 不 畀).

In two cases *shang* can even be considered as referring to the deity.[12] The greatness of Heaven is more commonly affirmed by the combination *huangtian* (fourteen occurrences), in two cases *mintian* and in one case *haotian*. One might wonder whether the addition of *huang* to *huangshangdi* (once) did not occur under the influence of the concept of *huangtian*. The fullest combination that occurs only once is *huangtianshangdi* (an expression also noticed by Yan Mo).[13]

Is there then no difference between *shangdi* and *tian*? Only one obvious difference appears from this statistical approach. While the concept of *tianming* (or other combinations of *tian* with *ming*) is well established, combinations of *di* or *shangdi* with *ming* are exceptional. We find this combination only six times: three times as *shangdiming*[14], once as *shangdi zhi gengming* (上 帝 之 耿 命)[15], once as *dizhiming* (帝 之 命)[16] and once more in a sentence[17]. This shows the different roles that are related to Heaven and Lord: except for these six references, the sending of a mandate is always attributed to Heaven. It can be noted that in several instances where *tian* and *shangdi* appear in the same context, their different roles are respected.[18] We have not yet found a sufficient explanation for this difference, but it could possibly be explained by the different roles Lord and Heaven played

---

[12] Jiugao (38), p.409: ...弗 惟 德 馨 香 祀 ， 登 聞 于 天 。 誕 惟 民 怨 ， 庶 群 自 酒 ， 腥 聞 在 上 ， 故 天 降 喪 于 殷 ...
Lüxing (55), p.592: ...方 告 無 辜 于 上 ， 上 帝 監 民.
[13] On this term see Granet, pp.64-65.
[14] Dagao (35), p.369: 己 予 惟 小 子 ， 不 敢 替 上 帝 命 ， 天 休 于 寧 王 ... "Yes, I, little child, dare not find fault with the command of the High Lord" ; p.373: 爽 邦 由 哲 ， 亦 惟 人 迪 知 上 帝 命 "If the faulty states would follow the wise man, there are the ten men who obey and understand the commands of the High Lord"; Junshi (44), p.475: 我 不 敢 寧 于 上 帝 命 ."I likewise dare not to be tranquil under the mandate of the High Lord".
[15] Lizheng (47), p.512: 亦 越 成 湯 ， 陟 丕 釐 上 帝 之 耿 命 "And now Cheng Tang, when he arose and regulated the brilliant mandate of the High Lord,...".
[16] Duofang (46), p.496: 厥 圖 帝 之 命 ..."Despising the Lord's command..."
[17] Kangwangzhigao (51), p.567:... 用 端 命 于 上 帝 ... "Thus did they receive) the true favouring decree from the High Lord".
[18] E.g.: Yiji (5), p.79: ...以 昭 受 上 帝 。 天 其 申 命 用 休 ; "...you will brightly receive [gifts from] the High Lord. Will not Heaven renew its favouring appointment, and give you blessing?"
Kangshi (37), p.385: ...聞 于 上 帝 ， 帝 休 ， 天 乃 大 命 文 王 ...; "it was heard by the High Lord, and the Lord favoured him. Heaven then gave the great order to Wen Wang (to kill the great Yin)": in this sentence one can consider the deities *(shang)di* and *tian* as interchangeable, but one can also consider them as different deities, or at least expressing the different roles attributed to one deity.

respectively in the Shang and Zhou.[19] Finally it can be observed that the concepts of *tiandao* and *tianzi*[20] are rarely used.[21]

6.2. The relationship between Heaven and human beings

Generally speaking there are only three actors in the relationship between Heaven and human beings:

1) Heaven (天) or High Lord (上 帝)
2) the sovereign (帝) or king (王) (or his substitute (duke (公) or prince (侯))
3) the people (民,下 民) (the expression *xiamin* in itself is interesting since it seems to stress the contrast between the "High Heaven" and the "low people").

It should be pointed out that the relationship between the three actors is not one of equality. There is clearly a privileged relationship between Heaven and the ruler, and without doubt Heaven or the Lord can be called the "King's God".[22] Most of the relationships between Heaven and the people are oriented towards the sovereign:

天 佑 下 民 ， 作 之 君 ， 作 之 師 ， 惟 其 克 相 上 帝 ， 寵 綏 四 方

"Heaven, to protect the inferior people, made for them rulers, and made for them instructors, that they may be aiding God, and secure the tranquillity of the four quarters of the empire."[23]

---

[19] For the role and function of *di*, see Fu (1984), pp.12-13; some researchers (especially C. de Harlee) insisted on the difference between the two deities: cf. Tien, p.61 seq.

[20] *Tianzi* is a Zhou invention that did not exist in the Shang: cf. Ren Jiyu, p.94.

[21] From all the above statistical remarks, very few significant differences between the Old and New Text versions can be deduced: the chapters with high theologal density are all in the New Text version; *shangtian* and *tiandao* only appear in the Old Text version chapters. Of the fifteen references to *di* (distinguished from *shangdi*) fourteen appear in New Text chapters. Of the six combinations of *(shang)di* with *ming*, five appear in New Text chapters. Since in all these cases the occurrences are so few, it is difficult to draw any definite conclusions. Compare also with the statistics given by Creel, pp.494-495: Creel says that "If *tian* was a Zhou deity, while *di* was not, we might expect that early Zhou literature would show more occurrences of the former than of the latter. And it does indeed."

[22] Eno (19901), p.23.

[23] Taishi (*shang*) (27), p.286 (cf. Mencius I B 3, different version: 。 。 。 惟 曰 其 助 上 帝 ， 寵 之 四 方); cf. Duofang (46), p.497: 天 惟 時 求 民 主: "Heaven seeks a ruler for the people"; Lüxing (55), p.609: 今 天 相 民 ， 作 配 在 下: "Now, when Heaven would aid the people, it has created a counterpart for itself here below (i.e. the king himself)".

欲王以小民受天永命

"I wish that the king through the small people may receive Heaven's eternal mandate."[24]

What can be observed further is that only the king has a relationship with heaven that has an *individual* character; the other human beings have a *collective* relationship ("people"). One should ask whether there is any other type of an individual actor? The answer is *no*, and there seems to be no exception to this principle. All the other actors that have some relationship with Heaven are collective groups that can be related to the category of either the king or of the people. The first are the "ministers" or "officers" who assist the king in his duty of serving Heaven.[25] The second are the "men or women", "the innocent" who cry to Heaven or in one case "the army" waiting for the decree of Heaven.[26]

6.3. The reactive Heaven

There are two major roles that can be attributed to Heaven: Heaven sends down its Mandate to the virtuous and Heaven punishes the evil. With regard to these functions, the passages that mention punishment (over 53) are more numerous than those about giving a Mandate (over 47).

In both cases, the general pattern is that of a *reactive* Heaven, which means that Heaven does not in an active way chose someone whom it will make virtuous so as to carry out the role of sovereign, but in reaction to the virtue (德) of a given person, Heaven gives its mandate. In the same way, Heaven does not punish or test an innocent or a good sovereign, Heaven punishes in a reactive way the one who has committed crimes (罪) and done a lot of evil. We can give a few examples of reactive Heaven:

---

[24] Shaogao (40), p.433; see on the relationship between Heaven and the people also Fu (1984), p.32 seq..
[25] For instance: "ministers" or "officials" are supposed to help the sovereign to understand Heaven's majesty and to strengthen the decree of Heaven (see: Kanggao (38), p.388 (the king speaks to Feng); Shaogao (48), p.433 (Duke of Shao speaks to the king); Junshi (44), p.481; Duofang (46), p.503; see also the example of the "ten officers" in Dagao (35), p.373 (cf. note 23); in Lüxing (55), pp.597-598 "the directors of criminal cases" are said to have upheld Heaven's virtue; the king calls them, together with the managers of government "Heaven's pastors" (天牧).
[26] "Men and women" (士女) in Wucheng (31), p.314; "the innocent" (無辜) (as a universal "everybody who is innocent") in Taishi (*zhong*), (28), p.290; "the army" (師) in Wucheng (31), p.314.

The first reaction is related to virtue and could be summarized in the expression: 天命有德: "Heaven gives charges to those who have virtue".[27] This means that one first needs to have virtue, before receiving a mandate of Heaven. It is noteworthy that in many passages of the *Book of Documents*, one first finds a description of virtue and only then the reaction of Heaven.

文王克明德慎罰。不敢侮鰥寡，庸庸，祗祗
，威威，顯民。。。聞于上帝，帝休，天乃
大命文王，殪戎殷，誕受厥命。。。"

King Wen was able to make bright the virtue and to be careful about the punishments. He dared not maltreat the widowers and widows. Very meritorious, very respectful, very majestic, he was illustrious among the people... it was seen and heard by the High Lord, and the Lord favoured him. Heaven then gave the great order to king Wen to kill the great Yin and grandly receive its mandate."[28]

In this passage, one first has a description of the virtue of king Wen; his fame ascends to the High Lord, who only then approves, and Heaven extends his Mandate. In the Junshi (44), one finds a passage very similar to this one: first the description of the virtue of king Wen and the help he received from his ministers in the cultivation of this virtue and the knowledge of the dread majesty of Heaven (知天威); then his fame ascends to the High Lord and he receives the Mandate (聞于上帝，惟時受有殷命哉).[29] A similar reaction can be found in the Dayumo (3) concerning the choice of Yu:

益曰：都，帝德廣運，乃聖乃神，乃武乃文
，皇天眷命，奄有四海，爲天下君.

"Oh! your virtue, O Emperor, is vast and incessant. It is sage, spiritual, awe-inspiring, and adorned with all accomplishments. Great Heaven regarded you with its favouring decree and suddenly you obtained all within the four seas, and became sovereign of the empire."[30]

In the same text, one also finds Yi saying to Yu: 惟德動天 "It is virtue which moves Heaven".[31]

---

[27] Gaoyaomo (4), p.74.
[28] Kanggao (37), p.383-385.
[29] Junshi (44), pp.480-482.
[30] Dayumo (3), p.54.
[31] ibidem, p.65.

The second type of reaction is related to evil: This can be summarized in the expression: 天 討 有 罪 "Heaven punishes those who have guilt"[32]. In this type of reaction, one first finds the description of evil done by the sovereign, then the punishment imposed by Heaven and change of its mandate.

A nice example can be found in the Jiugao (38). After a description of the alcoholic addiction of the last king of Yin, and of its damaging effects, the text continues:

… 弗 惟 德 馨 香 祀 ， 登 聞 于 天 ， 誕 惟 民 怨 ， 庶 群 自 酒 ， 腥 聞 在 上 ， 故 天 降 喪 于 殷 ， 罔 愛 于 殷 ， 惟 逸 ， 天 非 虐 ， 惟 民 自 速 辜

"…It was not (so) that fragrant offerings (made with) virtue ascended and were perceived by Heaven; the people were very resentful and the crowds intoxicated themselves, and the rank smell was perceived on high. Therefore, when Heaven sent down destruction on Yin and had no love for Yin it was due to (his) excesses. Heaven is not tyrannical, people themselves draw guilt upon themselves."[33]

Here we have a similar pattern as the above quotation on giving a mandate, with the inclusion of the ascent of the fame to Heaven. The reactive element is stressed in the conclusion where it is said the "Heaven is not tyrannical, people themselves draw guilt upon themselves."

Examples of both reactions (mandate and punishment) can be found in a long passage of Shaogao (40)[34]. There it is explained that reverence to virtue (敬 德)[35] results in the acceptance of the Mandate (受 天 命), and in the guidance (迪) and protection (保) of Heaven; no reverence (不 敬 德) makes the Mandate to fall down (墜 命). Another example of both aspects can be found in the Yixun (13):

---

[32] Gaoyaomo (4), p.74.
[33] Jiugao (38), p.409.
[34] Shaogao (40), pp.425-433.
[35] On this term see also Chen Xiyong, pp.84-85.

古 有 夏 先 后 ， 方 懋 厥 德 ， 罔 有 天 災 。。。其
子 孫 弗 率 ， 皇 天 降 災．"

Of old, the earlier sovereigns of Xia earnestly cultivated their virtue, and
then there were no calamities from Heaven... But their descendants did
not follow [their example], and Great Heaven sent down calamities."[36]

And the instruction of Yi concludes:

惟 上 帝 不 常 ， 作 善 降 之 百 祥 ， 作 不 善 降 之 百
殃

"[The ways of] the High Lord are not invariable: on the good-doer He
sends down all blessings, and on the evil-doer He sends down all
miseries."[37]

In the last quotation the action is attributed to the High Lord. Earlier
we have noticed that there are only a few instances where the Lord is actually
giving a mandate. It can be noticed here that the cases where the Lord or
High Lord punishes are also relatively few. It seems that the Lord pays an
even more passive role than Heaven. In the quotations we mentioned, we have
seen that the rumours of good or evil reach the Lord but that Heaven is the
initiator of the reaction. The dominant passive role of High Lord can be
confirmed by the fact that fewer cases of sacrifices or offerings are related to
the High Lord rather than to Heaven.[38]

*Should one therefore conclude that there is no active role for Heaven
with regard to giving a mandate or imposing punishment?* [Other types of
activities, not directly related to these aspects will be treated later] In fact we
can find a few examples of Heaven actively searching in order to give his
Mandate, and also a few examples of Heaven imposing punishment without
reason.

---

[36] Yixun (13), pp.193-194.

[37] ibidem, p.198; compare with the very similar sentence in Tanggao (12), p.186: 天 道 福
善 禍 淫 ， 降 災 于 夏 ， 以 彰 厥 罪 :"The way of Heaven is to bless the good and to
punish the bad. It sent down calamities on [the Hours of] Xia, to make manifest its crimes",
On the meaning of 不 常 see Fu (1984), pp.60-64.

[38] Shundian (2), p.33 : 肆 類 于 上 帝 "He sacrificed especially, but with the ordinary
forms, to the High Lord"; Taishi (*shang*) (27), p.287: 類 于 上 帝 : "I offered special
sacrifice to the High Lord" (on *lei*, see Tien, pp.69-70); Weizizhiming (36), pp.378-379: 上
帝 時 歆 : "The High Lord will always enjoy your offerings". Heaven see: Jiugao (38), p.409:
弗 惟 得 馨 香 祀 ， 登 聞 于 天 :"It was not [so] that fragrant offerings [made with]
virtue ascended and were perceived by Heaven"; Duofang (46), p.501: 惟 典 神 天 : "... to
preside over all services to spirits and to Heaven" (compare Fu (1984), p.66 seq.).

There are only three cases where Heaven is actively searching (求) for a virtuous king. In the Duofang (46), it is related how the king of Xia lost his mandate and was punished by Heaven as a result of his bad conduct (reactive). "Heaven then sought a new lord for the people, and grandly it sent down its illustrious and felicitous mandate to Cheng Tang" (天 惟 時 求 民 主 ， 乃 大 降 顯 休 命 于 成 湯)[39]. The same happened with the last king of Yin (reactive), and "Heaven then searched in your numerous regions" (天 惟 求 爾 多 方). Only the king of Zhou took care of the people, and was able to use virtue (用 德) :

天 惟 式 敎 我 用 休 ， 簡 畀 殷 命 ， 尹 爾 多 方

"Heaven then instructed us to avail ourselves of its grace, it selected us and gave us Yin's mandate, to rule over your numerous regions."[40]

One finds a very similar text in the Xianyouyide (17): The king of Xia was not able to use virtue (庸 德) and oppressed the people:

皇 天 弗 保 ， 監 于 萬 方 ， 啓 迪 有 命 ， 眷 求 一 德 ， 俾 作 神 主 ， 惟 尹 躬 曁 湯 ， 咸 有 一 德 ， 可 享 天 心 ， 受 天 明 命

"Great Heaven no [longer] extended its protection to him. It looked out among the myriad regions to give its guidance to one who might receive its favour, fondly seeking [a possessor] of pure virtue, whom it might make lord of the spirits. [Then] there were I, Yin, and Tang, both possessed of pure virtue, and able to satisfy the mind of Heaven. He received the bright favour of Heaven..."[41]

As can be observed from these texts, there is an interplay between reaction and action. The active part lies only in the search for a new king, who has to have virtue in order to receive the Mandate.

There are also three examples of Heaven punishing without giving a prior reason:

In the Jinteng (34), it is related how "in the autumn, when there was great ripeness, when they had not yet reaped, Heaven made great thunder

---

[39] Duofang (46), p.497.
[40] Ibidem, p.501-502.
[41] Xianyouyide (17), pp.214-215; 監 also expresses a more active part, compare with Lüxing (55), p.592 where "the High Lord surveyed the people" (上 帝 監 民), but there was no fragrant virtue, the smell sent out by the punishments was rank.

and rain with wind (天 大 雷 電 以 風), all the grain laid itself down, great trees then were uprooted. The people of the land greatly feared."[42]

At the beginning of Dagao (35) one finds: 天 降 割 于 我 家 不 少 延: "The merciless Heaven sends down injury on our house, without the slightest delay."[43]

Finally in the Guming (50), king Jing feeling the end of his life approaching says 今 天 降 疾 "Now Heaven has sent down a sickness that is fatal."[44]

It can be noticed that in the first text the reaction of Heaven is interpreted as signalizing the virtue of the Duke of Zhou. Once king Jing goes out to meet the Duke of Zhou, "Heaven sent down rain, and by virtue of a contrary wind, the grain all rose up". Moreover, the last cases are not historical narratives but words put in the mouth of a king (who has the mandate), applying it to himself or to his house. In the second text the focus is that Heaven has taken away his Mandate from Yin and given it to Zhou and will not change his mind. But still no real reason is given for the terrors that are attributed to Heaven, apart from the fact that "the small ruler of Yin, knows that our state has a flaw and that the people are not tranquil." The whole event seems to be interpreted as a warning to be faithful to the decree of Heaven. In the third text, though the king has applied Heaven's majesty and adhered to the instructions of king Wen and Wang (敬 迓 天 威 ， 嗣 守 文 武 大 訓), he fell ill and attributes his illness to Heaven. His death, however, does not result in the loss of the Mandate for his son. The three stories (New Text chapters) all relate episodes from the beginning of the Western Zhou when, as is generally admitted, Heaven had not yet become a royal adversary. But, in these cases, even if no prior reason for Heaven's conduct is given, Heaven is not accused of being unjust or unkind.[45]

6.4. The bright Heaven and majestic Heaven

The first "definition" of Heaven in the *Book of Documents* can be found in the Gaoyaomo (4), following the two citations we mentioned earlier:

---

[42] Jinteng (34), p.359.
[43] Dagao (35), p.362.
[44] Guming (50), p.548.
[45] Cf. Fu, p.73; Eno (1990a), p.24-27.

天聰明自我民聰明，天明畏自我民明威.

"Heaven's hearing and seeing proceed from our people's hearing and seeing. Heaven's enlightenment and fearsomeness proceed from our people's enlightenment and severity."[46]

This quotation contains two characteristics of Heaven which are linked together: Heaven is bright (明) and Heaven is majestic or fearsome (畏). In two other passages one finds a similar combination: In the Dagao (35) it is said: 天 明 畏: "Heaven is bright and majestic"[47]; and in Duoshi (42): 惟 我 下 民 秉 爲 ， 惟 天 明 畏: "What our people held to and did, that was (the expression of) Heaven's discernment and severity"[48]. It appears that these two characteristics are linked to the two major roles of Heaven: brightness is connected with mandating and fearsomeness with punishing.

In fact one can establish a number of paradigm clusters around those two characteristics and functions.

We have already seen the relationship between the Mandate or Heaven and the virtue of the sovereign. Of this virtue it is often said that it is "bright" or "illustrious", and also that the sovereign through his actions makes his virtue bright (明 德).[49] It can be noticed that in an associative way the mandate is called bright as well (明 命)[50]. Another word that is used for the brightness of the sovereign is 顯,[51] and in a similar associative way, this term is related to Heaven.[52] With "brightness" or "clearness" we are not only in an

---

[46] Gaoyaomo (40), p.74.

[47] Dagao (35), p.369.

[48] Duoshi (42), p.455.

[49] See e.g. Kanggao (37), p.381: 惟 乃 丕 顯 考 文 王 克 明 德 慎 罰 "Your greatly illustrious [dead] father king Wen was able to make bright the virtue and to be careful about the punishments"; see also: Zicai (39), pp.417-418; Shaogao (40), p.433; Duoshi (42), pp.456-457; Junshi (44), p.476; Duofang (46), p.498; Junchen (49), p.539; Lüxing (55), p.593; Wenhouzhiming (56), p.613.

[50] Taijia (shang) (14), p.199: 先 王 顧 諟 天 之 明 命 :"The former king kept his eye continually on the bright requirements of Heaven"; Xianyouyide (17), p.215: 受 天 明 命 : "He received the bright favour of Heaven".

[51] Wenhouzhiming (56), p.613: 丕 顯 文 武 克 慎 明 德 "The greatly illustrious Wen and Wu could be careful to make bright the virtue..." and further in the same chapter, p.619: 用 成 爾 顯 德 "...and thus achieve your illustrious virtue"; see also example in note 55; Jiugao (38), pp.407-408; Luogao (41), p.443.

[52] Duofang (46), p.497 (example in main text quoted at note 45); Jiugao (38), p.407: 在 昔 殷 先 哲 王 ， 迪 畏 天 顯 小 民 : "In ancient times Yin's former wise kings in their conduct stood in awe of Heaven's clearness [=clear laws] and of the small people"; Duoshi (42), p.457: 罔 顧 于 天 顯 民 祗 :"...he had no consideration for Heaven's clearness, nor for the respect due to the people".

aesthetic paradigm, but also in a paradigm of knowledge. One of the roles of the sovereign, therefore, is to "understand" the Mandate of Heaven. Yet, the ultimate ideal is that the sovereign "complies with" (配) Heaven. At this point one may ask whether there is any affective relationship between Heaven and the sovereign to whom it gives its mandate (earlier we have seen that there is one between Heaven and the people). In fact, this affective relationship is very limited. There is only one negative sentence in which "love", or better "care" is mentioned: 天 降 喪 于 殷 ， 罔 愛 于 殷: "Heaven sent down destruction on Yin and had no love for Yin".[53] In one other instance Heaven shows its kindness to the people (天 惠 民)[54] or its compassion for the people (哀)[55] The general pattern is that of a more distant "favouring its Mandate" (or "giving grace" to a king) (休)[56], of assisting (佑) the sovereign or the people.[57]

The other characteristic of Heaven is its severity or majesty. Here also one can establish a paradigm cluster. The dominant character is that of *wei* 威: it not only refers to an awe-inspiring majesty, but also to the "terror" implied in punishment. Once more the relationship with the sovereign can be established: of a sovereign who neglects the Mandate it is often said that he tyrannizes (作 威) over his people, and this term is always used in a fierce context.[58] As a result of this action, Heaven also sends down its terrors (天 降 威)[59]. It is also up to the sovereign to display the majesty of Heaven.[60] With regard to the possibility of such a terrifying Heaven, the corresponding attitude of the sovereign is one of awe (畏): 永 畏 惟 罰 "You should ever stand in awe of the punishment [of Heaven]".[61] There are several other words

---

[53] Jiugao (38), p.409; another affective expression could be 斐 忱 or the "sincere assistance" given by Heaven. However the translation of this expression is uncertain; it can also be translated as "Heaven cannot be relied upon" as Kalgren does (Dagao (35), p.370, 373; Kanggao (29), p.387: 天 畏 斐 忱 ; Junshi (44), p.475).
[54] Taishi (*shang*) (27), p.290.
[55] Shaogao (40), p.426; after that the people cried with compassion to Heaven (以 哀 籲 天); notice that the "heart" (心), is only twice connected with *shangdi* (Tanggao (12), p.189) or *tian*.(Xianyouyide (17), p.215).
[56] E.g, Dagao (35), p.369.
[57] E.g. Junshi (44), p.479 (mandate); Tanggao (12), p.188 (people); also 保 cf. Xianyouyide (17), p.214.
[58] Tanggao (12), p.186: 夏 王 滅 德 作 威 ， 以 敷 虐 于 爾 萬 方 百 姓 "The king of Xia extinguished his virtue and played the tyrant, extending his oppression over you, the people of the myriad regions."; see also: Taishi (*xia*) (29), p.295-296; Hongfan (32), p.334; Kanggao (37), p.395.
[59] Dagao (35), p.366; see also ibidem, p.364; Xibokanli (25), p.271; Jinteng (34), p.300.
[60] Tanggao (12), p.187; Taishi (*shang*) (27), p.285; Duoshi (42), p.454.
[61] Lüxing (55), p.610; see also: Tangshi (10), p.174; Jiugao (38), p.406 (see note 58).

that express this attitude of reverence and awe: *yan* (嚴)[62], *jing* (敬)[63], *gong* (恭)[64]. The following quote is a very good example of the sovereign's attitude:

昔 在 殷 王 中 宗 ， 嚴 恭 寅 畏 ， 天 命 自 度 ， 制 民
祗 懼

"In ancient times, Yin's king Zhong Zong was dignified, respectful, reverent and fearful. By [the norms of] Heaven's commands he measured himself, through the respect due to the people he felt awed."[65]

Also in this register, the affective language is very limited: the clearest examples are those of Heaven expressing its anger: 天 震 怒 [66] and 帝 乃 震 怒.[67]

6.5. Conclusion

The most important conclusion of this analysis is that in the theology of the *Book of Documents*, the sovereign not only has a privileged relationship with Heaven, but he is the only one to have an individual relationship with Heaven. Heaven's communication with the people, always taken as a collective, is oriented towards a relationship with the king. Moreover, Heaven plays a reactive role of sending down its mandate to the virtuous and punishing the evil. Here the dominant characteristic is that of an awe-inspiring majesty.

---

[62] Lüxing (55), p.604: 具 嚴 天 威 :"You should all stand in awe of Heaven's majesty"
[63] Guming (50), p.545: 在 後 之 侗 ， 敬 迓 天 威 : "[I] the succeeding stupid one, have respectfully applied Heaven's majesty" p.559: 以 敬 忌 天 威 : "... reverently stand in awe of Heaven"; Taishi (*shang*) (27), p.284: 今 商 王 受 ， 弗 敬 上 天 ， 降 災 下 民 : "Now, Shou, the king of Shang, does not reverence Heaven above, and inflicts calamities on the people below."; see also: Luogao (41), pp.437-438; Duoshi (42), p.462; Lüxing (55), p.600.
[64] Ganshi (7), p.153: 今 予 惟 恭 行 天 之 罰 : "Now I am reverently executing the punishment appointed by Heaven"; see also very similar expressions in Taishi (*xia*) (29), p.296: 恭 行 天 罰 and in Mushi (30), p.304: 惟 恭 行 天 之 罰 ; see also Wucheng (31), p.313: 恭 天 成 命 : "Reverently obeying the determinate counsel of Heaven".
[65] Wuyi (43), p.466.
[66] Tangshi (*shang*) (27), p.285.
[67] Hongfan (32), p.323.

102

Chapter 7: The *Book of Odes*

7.1. Statistical analysis

As the result of the identification of all passages related to the deities "Heaven" and "Lord", the following list was established.

tian (天): 92
shangtian (上 天): 3
huangtian (皇 天): 2
haotian (昊 天): 22
mintian (旻 天): 3
cangtian (蒼 天): 8
tianming (天 命): 9
tianzi (天 子): 22
tianxia (天 下): 1

di (帝): 13
shangdi (上 帝): 19
huang(yi)shangdi (皇 (矣) 上 帝): 3
haotianshangdi (昊 天 上 帝): 3
(shang)diming (上 帝 命): 5

In total 73 poems (i.e. 1/3 of the total number of poems) have a reference to *tian* or *shangdi*[1]: in fact, this number is to be reduced by about 17 if one excludes the poems where *tian* clearly means "sky", or where it is

---

[1] Texts traditionally dating from the Western Zhou (1122-770 B.C.) (Zhousong: early Western Zhou; Daya and Xiaoya: middle and late period of Western Zhou) are more theologal than those dating from a more recent period (Lusong and Shangsong: early Eastern Zhou (770-256) and Guofeng: early Eastern Zhou). For these dates, see Fu, pp.25-26.

Terms in the *Book of Odes*

Ode	帝	上帝	皇矣上帝	昊天上帝	上帝命	天	上天	皇天	旻天	昊天	蒼天	天命	天子	天下
40						3								
45						2								
47	1					1								
65											3			
118						1								
121											3			
131						3								
155						1								
166						4								
168													2	
177						1							1	
178						1							2	
180						1								
184						1								
191						1			5				1	
192			1			4								
193						1						1		
194						1			2	1			1	

Ode	天下	天子	天命	蒼天	旻天	昊天	皇天	上天	天	上帝命	昊天上帝	皇矣上帝	上帝	帝
195														
196									1					
197			1		1				2					
198						3								
199									1					
200				2										
202						1								
203									2					
204									1					
205									1					
207								1	1					
210								1	1					
215														
222		4												
224									1				2	
229									1					
235			2					1	2	1			2	1
236									6				2	
238									1					

Ode	帝	上帝	皇矣上帝	昊天上帝	上帝命	天	上天	皇天	昊天	旻天	蒼天	天命	天子	天下
239						1								
241	8	1	2			1								1
243						3								
245	1	2												
247						1								
249						2							1	
252		1				1							1	
254						7			2					
255		3				3								
256						1		1	2					
257						3			1					
258		1		3		2			2					
259						1								
260						2							2	
262													3	
263													2	
264						4			2					
265						2								
266										1				

Ode	帝	上帝	皇矣上帝	昊天上帝	上帝命	天	上天	皇天	旻天	昊天	蒼天	天命	天子	天下
267						1								
270						1						1		
271									1					
272						2			1					
273									1					
274		1												
275					1	1								
276		1								1				
282								1					1	
288						1								
294						1						1		
296						1								
300	1	2				2								
302						1								
303	1	1			1							1		
304					2	2							1	1
305												2		
Total	13	19	3	3	5	92	3	2	22	22	8	9	22	1

related to celestial bodies, or in which only the term Son of Heaven (*tianzi*) appears.[2]

As in the *Book of Documents*, the dominant concept is that of *tian*, but in proportion there are more references to *(shang)di*. In the *Book of Odes*, *tian* seems to be interchangeable with *shangdi*: the clearest example is poem 235 in which the terms 天, 上 天, 天 命, 帝 命, 上 帝 appear. There is also great variety in terms of prefixes: *huangtian* (皇 天), *haotian* (昊 天), *mintian* (旻 天), *cangtian* (蒼 天), *huang(yi) shangdi* (皇 (矣) 上 帝) and three times in one poem the longest combination *haotian shangdi* (昊 天 上 帝) (ode 258).[3]

With regard to other combinations, there are some clear differences from the *Book of Documents*: there are more mentions of the concept of the Son of Heaven (天 子) (in total 23) than in the *Book of Documents* (in total 7); there is only one mention of *tianxia* (天 下)[4], and no reference to *tiandao* (天 道)[5]. Finally, there are only 7 references to *tianming* (天 命), whereas there are at least five combinations of *(Shang)di* with *ming*[6]. The few mentions of the "mandate of Heaven" can partially be explained by the literary genre of the poems, which are less political or historical than the *Book of Documents*. Finally, the term *di* (帝), always has the meaning of deity, it never appears in the sense of sovereign.[7]

7.2. The relationship between Heaven and human beings

In the *Book of Odes*, we find again the three actors in the relationship between Heaven and human beings: 1) Heaven or Lord; 2) the sovereign; and 3) the people. In ode 241, we find a nice example in which the three actors are involved in their specific roles: the Lord seeking a sovereign to guide and protect the people:

---

[2] "Sky": 118, 155, 178, 196 (+*tianzi*), 204, 205, 239, 249 (+*tianzi*), 252 (+*tianzi*), 254; "celestial bodies": 203, 238; *tianzi*: 168, 177, 196 (+sky), 222, 249 (+sky), 252 (+sky), 262, 263.

[3] According to Tien (p.50-51), the choice of *tian* or *di*, or the addition of prefixes was much influenced by the rhythm and the harmony of tones of the odes.

[4] In ode 241,5.

[5] This is a relatively late term, cf. Ren, chap 3.

[6] 帝 命 : 235, 275, 303, 304 (2x); 上 帝 既 命 : 235.

[7] See also Tien, p.79.

108

皇 矣 上 帝 。 。 。 求 民 之 莫 。 。 。 天 立 厥 配 。
。 。 文 王 其 德 靡 悔 ， 既 受 地 祉

"August is the High Lord ... he sought tranquillity for the people ...
Heaven established for itself a counterpart [on earth], ... King Wen, his
virtue had nothing that caused regret; he received Lord's blessings."[8]

In the analysis of the *Book of Documents* we have noticed that only
the sovereign had a relationship with Heaven that has an individual character.
In the *Book of Odes*, we find a different pattern. This is due to the particular
genre of the odes related to Heaven, which can be called "odes of
lamentation". In these poems an anonymous poet addresses his complaints to
Heaven. There are cases, where the sovereign himself complains[9], but in most
other cases it is probably a noble or officer; in any case not the sovereign
himself, who laments about the misery of the country and the misfortunes
sent down by Heaven. In some odes, the contents are more specific, as for
instance a son who cannot bury his parents[10] or the queen who is degraded[11].
Because most of these odes are anonymous, it is sometimes very difficult to
guess the context and therefore the author.[12]

The relationship between the author and Heaven as expressed in these
odes is of a different nature:

1) The author addresses his complaint to Heaven, without having a
particular relationship with Heaven: for instance the complaint of a eunuch:

驕 人 好 好 ， 勞 人 草 草 ， 蒼 天 蒼 天 ， 視 彼 驕 人
， 矜 此 勞 人

"The arrogant men are pleased, the toiling men are anxious; blue
Heaven, blue Heaven, look at those arrogant men, pity these toiling
men!"[13]

2) The author makes a descriptive statement about Heaven, such as
that the disorder is caused by Heaven or that Heaven is changeable; here also
there is no particular relationship between the author and Heaven:

---

[8] Ode 241,5; see another example in ode 254, where an officer addresses himself to the king.
[9] Cf. ode 258.
[10] Ode 202.
[11] Ode 229.
[12] See for instance ode 199, which could be the complaint by the prince of Su, who had been
slandered by the prince of Bao; but it can also be that a lady complains that the gentleman she
loves is unfaithful (cf. Kalgren (1950), p.149).
[13] Ode 200.

"The wide and great Heaven, it does not prolong its grace; it sends down death and famine; it destroys and strikes the states of the four quarters; Great Heaven is terrific, it does not ponder, it does not plan; it cares not about those who have guilt, they have already undergone their punishment; even such as these who have no guilt are all made to suffer together."[14]

3) Finally there are cases where the author himself/herself is affected: the heir-apparent bewailing his degradation says: 我 獨 于 罹 ，何 辜 于 天 ，我 最 伊 何 "I alone am in misery; what guilt have I against Heaven, what is my offense?"[15]; in ode 257, the author says: 逢 天 僤 怒 "I have met with the ample anger of Heaven".[16]

These examples, then, are clearly different from what appears in the *Book of Documents*. Yet, there is one very clear example of a particular relationship between Heaven and a human being other than the sovereign: lady Yuan of Jiang (姜 嫄), mother of Hou Ji (后 稷), who was made fruitful by the Lord; she is said to have first borne the tribe of Zhou[17]. Hou Ji himself became later a counterpart of Heaven (克 配 彼 天).[18]

7.3. The reactive Heaven

The two major roles attributed to Heaven, sending down its Mandate to the virtuous and punishing the evil can be found in the *Book of Odes* as well.

With regard to the blessings, the general pattern is also that of a reactive Heaven, or they are at least related to the virtue (德) of the king. Ode 241, which has already been quoted above, is a typical example:

> Now this king Wen, God probed his heart: settled was his reputation, in his virtue he was able to be enlightened (其 德 克 明); he was able to be enlightened, to be good; he was able to preside, to be ruler, to be king over this great kingdom; he was able to be accommodating, to be in harmony [with his subjects]; and when they

---

[14] Ode 194,1; see also sections of odes 191, 192, 195, 198, 224, 264, 265.
[15] Ode 197,1.
[16] Ode 257,4. or another example, see ode 40: "I am straitened indeed and poor, nobody understands my difficulties; it is all over, Heaven truly has done it (天 實 為 之)."
[17] Odes 245 and 300.
[18] Ode 275. In ode 47, we find another relationship between a woman and Heaven, where the wife of the sovereign is compared to heaven and the Lord: 胡 然 而 天 也 ， 胡 然 而 帝 也 ： "How is she so like Heaven, how is she so like the Lord?"; this, however, is only a comparative relationship.

110

were in harmony with king Wen, his virtue had nothing that caused regret; he received God's blessings; it reached to his grandsons and sons."[19]

The dominant pattern, however, is that of a punishing Heaven. The examples are many:

彼 蒼 者 天 ， 殱 我 良 人

"That blue Heaven, it destroys our good men."[20]

天 方 薦 瘥 ， 喪 亂 弘 多 。 。 。 昊 天 不 傭 ， 降 此
鞠 訩 ， 昊 天 不 惠 ， 降 此 大 戾

"Heaven now repeatedly causes epidemics, death and disorders are widespread and many ... The Great Heaven is not just, it sends down these ample quarrels; the great Heaven is not kind, it sends down these great transgressions."[21]

天 夭 是 椓

"Heaven's killing strikes them."[22]

浩 浩 昊 天 ， 不 駿 其 德 ， 降 喪 饑 饉

"The wide and Great Heaven, it does not prolong its grace; it sends down death and famine."[23]

"Oh, distant, Great Heaven, you are called father and mother; there is no offense, there is not guilt, but the disorder (亂) is as great as this! Great Heaven is very terrific, but I truly committed no offense; great Heaven is tremendous, but I truly have no guilt."[24]

天 步 艱 難 ， 之 子 不 猶

"Heaven's course is calamitous; this gentleman is no good."[25]

---

[19] Other examples in odes 243, 247, 249, 274, 304.
[20] Ode 131.
[21] Ode 191.
[22] Ode 192,13.
[23] Ode 194,1.
[24] Ode 198,1.
[25] Ode 229,2.

上帝板板，下民卒瘅。○○○天之方難。○○○
天之方虐。○○○天之方懠

"The High Lord has become stern, and the lower people are full of
distress. ... Heaven now causes calamities ... Heaven is now oppressive
... Heaven is now angry."[26]

何辜今之人，天降喪亂，饑饉薦臻。○○○旱
既大甚。○○○後稷不克，上帝不臨，耗斁下
土，寧丁我躬

"Alas, what guilt rests on the present men? Heaven sends down death
and disorder, famine comes repeatedly ... The drought is excessive ...
but Hou Ji is powerless, and High Lord does not favour us; he wastes
and destroys the earth below; why does he strike us?"[27]

I look up to the great Heaven, but it is not kind to us; for a long time
we have not had peace, it has sent down these great evils; in the state
nothing is settled, officers and people suffer; nocuous insects gnaw and
injure, there is no peace, no moderation, the guilty ones are not
apprehended; there is no peace, no cure ... disorder is not sent down
from Heaven, it is produced by women; those who cannot be taught or
instructed are women and eunuchs ... Why does Heaven reprove you,
why do the Spirits not bless you?"[28]

Here we meet with a new type of punishment. In the *Book of
Documents*, punishment had a political function. Heaven sends down
calamities on a bad sovereign, so that a change of Heavenly Mandate may
occur. This was the explanation of the creation of the Zhou dynasty. In the
Book of Odes, however, this punishment is rarely related to a change of
mandate. It is presented as a lamentation by someone who suffers from the
punishment but who is not the cause of the crimes committed. Several of
these odes may date from after the fall of the western capital. The original
cause of evil may be the bad sovereign[29], the palace women and eunuchs[30] or
the unfaithful lover[31], but in several cases the cause is not clear[32] and only a
complaint can be addressed to Heaven. This is the birth of the unjust Heaven,
a sky god, that is terrifying, unjust and blind. Robert Eno has correctly put
forward the new characteristic of Heaven: "In these poems, a clear distinction
is drawn between human evil, which is caused by man, and the chaos that

---

[26] Ode 254.
[27] Ode 258.
[28] Ode 264; other examples in odes 255 (due to the sovereign, not to Heaven), 256, 257, 265.
[29] Ode 191.
[30] Ode 264.
[31] Ode 229.
[32] Ode 258.

112

engulfs the innocent, caused by *Tian*. Guilt is assigned to man in the former case, but to *Tian* in the latter."[33]

7.4. The bright Heaven and majestic Heaven

As in the *Book of Documents* we meet with a bright and majestic Heaven: a concise example can be found in ode 236:

明 明 在 下 ， 赫 赫 在 上 ， 天 難 忱 斯

"Shedding brightness below, majestic on high, it is difficult to rely on Heaven."[34]

Heaven or Lord are called bright: 明 明 上 天 "Bright is the high Heaven"[35], 明 昭 上 帝 "Bright is the High Lord"[36]. They seek a counterpart on earth (配) who, like king Wen, is also called bright (昭, 顯, 明)[37]. Here also, the affective relationship between Heaven and the sovereign or the people is very limited, and often expressed in negative terms:

倬 彼 昊 天 ， 寧 不 我 矜

"Grand is that great Heaven, why does it not have pity on us?"[38]

瞻 卬 昊 天 ， 則 不 我 惠

"I look up to the great Heaven, but it is not kind to us."[39]

A closer relationship between the High Lord and the sovereign can be seen in the expression 上 帝 臨 女 "The High Lord approaches (=looks down upon) you"[40] even if this can also be an expression of the Lord's majesty as in ode 241: 皇 矣 上 帝 ， 臨 下 有 赫 "August is the High Lord; looking down, he is majestic."[41]

---

[33] Eno (1990a), p.27.
[34] Ode 236,1.
[35] Ode 207,1.
[36] Ode 276; see also ode 256.
[37] Odes 235 and 241; ee also ode 275.
[38] Ode 257,1.
[39] Ode 264,1.
[40] Odes 236,7 and 300,7.
[41] Ode 241,1.

Besides being bright, Heaven is also "majestic", and this characteristic appears in several of the odes of lamentation: 旻 天 疾 威 "Great Heaven is terrific"[42]. The emotional expression is "anger" (怒)[43]. As in the *Book of Documents*, the corresponding attitude of the people or the sovereign is that of "awe", "fear" or "reverence":

我 其 夙 夜 ， 畏 天 之 威 ， 于 時 保 之

"May we night and day fear the majesty of Heaven, and thereby preserve it [=what Heaven has conferred]."[44]

維 此 文 王 ， 小 心 翼 翼 ， 昭 事 上 帝

"Now this king Wen, he was careful and reverent, brightly he served the High Lord."[45]

A good summary of the two aspects of Heaven, with some of the corresponding attitudes, can be found in the following passage of ode 254:

敬 天 之 怒 ， 無 敢 戲 豫 ， 敬 天 之 渝 ， 五 敢 馳 驅 ， 昊 天 曰 明 ， 及 爾 出 王 ， 昊 天 曰 旦 ， 及 爾 游 衍

"Fear the anger of Heaven, do not dare to play and enjoy yourselves; fear the change of Heaven, do not dare to race about; Great Heaven is called bright: it observes your goings; Great Heaven is called clear-seeing, it observes your sporting and extravagances"[46].

Under this section we can mention one particular new aspect: of Heaven is said that "its actions have no sound and no smell" (上 天 之 載 ， 無 聲 無 臭)[47], and this is confirmed by the fact that Heaven never "speaks" in the *Book of Documents* or in the *Book of Odes*. There is only one exception: ode 241, where Lord directly speaks (謂) to King Wen[48].

---

[42] Odes 194, 195, 198, 255, 265.
[43] Ode 257.,4.
[44] Ode 272; see also odes 194 and 199: 不 畏 于 天 "You (he) does not [even] fear Heaven".
[45] Ode 236,3.
[46] Ode 254,8.
[47] Ode 235,7.
[48] Ode 241,5.

114

7.5. Conclusion

The most important conclusion of this section is that the *Book of Odes*, generally speaking, contains a theology that is quite similar to that of the *Book of Documents*, both in terms of the relationship between the three actors, as in terms of the contents of that relationship. But there is also a new element which appears in the odes of lamentation. People other than the sovereign address their complaints to Heaven, and Heaven appears in these odes as more terrifying.

Chapter 8: The *Analects*

8.1. Statistical analysis

    tian (天): 20
    tiandao (天 道): 1
    tianming (天 命): 3
    tianxia (天 下): 23
    tianzi (天 子): 2
    di (帝): 3

As can be observed, the number of references to *tian* or *di* in the *Analects* is very limited. Several aspects are worth noting. The most apparent is the total absence of the term *shangdi*. Moreover, the term *di* (all three references in *Analects* XX,1) only appears in what is supposed to be a quotation from the *Book of Documents*[1]. This seems to indicate that the term *tian* had become predominant in the period the *Analects* were compiled (the later Zhou dynasty). The term *tian* always appears as such and there are no examples with prefixes (such as *shangtian, huangtian*). Finally, the term *tianxia*, which was rarely used in the *Book of Documents* or the *Book of Odes*, has become a common word for the universe or kingdom in the *Analects*.

The limited number of occurrences makes it more difficult to develop a global analysis. However, some tendencies can be discerned. As in our analysis of the *Book of Documents* and the *Book of Odes*, we will continue to focus on the relationship between Heaven and the human being. This method is particularly useful for the *Analects* since they show less interest in what *Tian* in itself is, than how *Tian* deals with the human world.[2]

---

[1] Compare with Tanggao (<u>12</u>), pp.187-189: the difference mainly exists in the use of the terms *di*: the Analects writes 皇 皇 后 帝 whereas the Tanggao writes 上 天 神 后 ; the second *di* in the Analects is not to be found in Tanggao; for the third Tanggao writes 上 帝.
[2] Cf. Fu (1984), p.134.

8.2. The relationship between Heaven and human beings

We have noticed in the *Book of Documents* and the *Book of Odes* that three actors were involved in the relationship between Heaven and the human beings: 1) Heaven or Lord; 2) the sovereign; and 3) the people. In the *Analects* this relationship is quite radically altered. The breakthrough in the *Analects* with regard to the concept of Heaven, is a relationship *between Heaven and an individual other than the king or his substitutes*. Given the text's uncertain history, the *Analects* may not be original in this regard, but at least it reflects a breakthrough seen also in other texts of the Warring States.

The privileged relationship between the sovereign and Heaven is not abandoned in the *Analects*. The three references to *di*, which all appear in the same paragraph, refer to such a relationship. Of the twenty references to *tian* and three to *tianming*, however, only three refer directly to the relationship between the emperor (Yao or Shun) and Heaven[3]. Two other references establish the link between the relationship of Heaven and king Wen and its relationship with Confucius: Heaven has not destroyed the style of king Wen, it lives on in Confucius[4].

Yet, the dominant pattern is that of a relationship between Heaven and Confucius. This relationship is of a different nature.

The first form seems to be similar to the poems of lamentations which appeared in the *Book of Odes*. In the *Book of Odes*, most of these lamentations were anonymous. In the *Analects* the exclamations are voiced by Confucius' words: "May Heaven detest it!" (天 厭 之)[5] and "When Yan Yuan died, the Master said: 'Alas! Heaven is destroying me! Heaven is destroying me!' (天 喪 予)"[6]. The second of these exclamations is a clear example of a new relationship between Heaven and an individual other than the ruler. In both cases, however, one finds the idea of a terrifying and punishing Heaven, which is close to the one in the *Book of Odes*.

Under this category, two other more general exclamations by Confucius can be arranged: "Would I (we) be deceiving Heaven?" (欺 天 乎)[7] and "I do not murmur against Heaven..." (不 怨 天)[8]. Both of these ex-

---

[3] *Analects* VIII,19: "The Master said: 'Great indeed was Yao as a sovereign! How majestic was he! It is only Heaven that is grand, and only Yao corresponded to it. How vast [was his virtue]...'"; and XX,1: "Yao said: 'Oh! you, Shun, the Heaven-determined order of succession now rests in your person. Sincerely hold fast to the due Mean. If there shall be distress and want within the four seas, the Heavenly revenue will come to a perpetual end.'"

[4] *Analects* IX,5; for the interpretation of *wen* in this paragraph, we follow Eno, pp.84-85. We will follow his translation for several other sentences below.

[5] *Analects* VI,26 (two times).

[6] *Analects* XI,9.

[7] *Analects* IX,11.

[8] *Analects* XIV,35.

clamations present a human response to Heaven, here individualised in a particular person. There is also the exclamation: "Does Heaven speak?" (天 何 言 哉)[9] which underlines this individualisation. This is more than a simple exclamation. It is a comparison made by Confucius between himself and Heaven: in the same way as the four seasons pursue their courses and all things are continually being produced without Heaven speaking, Confucius also prefers not speaking. We have already encountered a Heaven that does not speak in the *Book of Odes*, but the new characteristic here is that a person other than the sovereign is compared with this Heaven.

However, the relationship between Heaven and Confucius is much more particular. Confucius says of himself that "Heaven has engendered virtue in me" (天 生 德 於 予)[10] and that "There is Heaven that knows me!" (知 我 者 其 天 乎)[11]. Other people also express this unique relationship: "Heaven is going to use your master as a bell with its wooden tongue" (天 將 以 夫 子 爲 木 鐸)[12] and "It is actually Heaven which allows him to be a great Sage..." (固 天 縱 之 將 聖)[13].

It is important to underline the difference between these sentences and the relationship between Heaven and the human being as it appears in the *Book of Documents* and the *Book of Odes*. In these Classics, one never finds a reference to Heaven choosing an individual other than the sovereign (to make him e.g. to a wooden bell). Moreover, one never finds Heaven engendering virtue in an individual other than the king. The only case in the *Book of Documents* where Heaven "engenders" (生), clearly shows the difference between the "people" (collective) and the "intelligent ruler" (individual): 惟 天 生 民 有 欲 ， 無 主 乃 亂 ； 惟 天 生 聰 明 時 叉: "Heaven engenders such desires in the people, that without a ruler they must fall into all disorders; and Heaven engenders the man of intelligence whose business it is to regulate them (or the disorder)"[14]. This comparison brings two other aspects to light. In *Book of Documents* and the *Book of Odes*, the Heavenly Mandate is given in reaction to a sovereign who already possesses virtue. Here the quotation of Heaven engendering virtue in Confucius does not appear within a context of reaction.[15] Confucius does not receive a Mandate but virtue itself. Moreover, the principal concept of the Mandate of Heaven in the previous Classics clearly includes the Mandate that the sovereign has to regulate the people. Here, the relationship with the people

---

[9] *Analects* XIX,25.
[10] *Analects* VII,23.
[11] *Analects* XIV,35.
[12] *Analects* III,24.
[13] *Analects* IX,6.
[14] Zhonghuizhigao (11), p.177-178.
[15] The reactive Heaven exists in the *Analects* only in the references to the sovereign and in VI,28: "The Master said: 'If I have done anything improper, may Heaven detest it (me).'"

has disappeared. In none of the cases in the *Analects* where a relationship between Heaven and Confucius exists, does the link with the people appear.

The new relationship can also be observed in Confucius' response to the relationship. "At fifty, I knew the Decree of Heaven" (五 十 而 知 天 命) [16]. Once more, in the entire *Book of Documents* or *Book of Odes*, one never finds a reference to an individual other than the sovereign knowing the Decree of Heaven. Only the sovereign "understood" Heaven. In this text a personalisation of the concept of *tianming* appears . The term no longer only has a political meaning, it becomes a personal decree, even a personal mission.[17]

In addition, this personal decree is not limited to Confucius himself. Among the three things a superior man (君 子) stands in awe of, is the Decree of Heaven (畏 天 命). The mean man, on the contrary, does not know the Decree of Heaven, and consequently does not stand in awe of it (小 人 不 知 天 命 而 不 畏 也)[18]. Here we face a new concept of the human being (the *junzi* is no longer the sovereign alone, but the cultivated human being), and therefore a new concept of Heaven (and Decree or Mandate) that will be fully developed in the *Mencius*. In this relationship between Heaven and the human being, it is remarkable that hardly any aspects of the "bright" Heaven have been preserved. The term "bright" never appears in connection with Heaven. The major attitude of the human being is one of "awe". While Heaven seems to have come closer to the human being due to the personal decree, the relationship has also become more distant.

The well-known sentence "He who offends against Heaven has none to whom he can pray" (獲 罪 於 天 ， 無 所 禱 也)[19] could possibly be interpreted within the context of this new relationship. A first reading could follow the traditional view on Heaven as appeared in the *Book of Documents* and the *Book of Odes*. *Zui* (罪), then, probably refers to the crimes committed by the sovereign against the people and therefore against Heaven. In such a case, the ruler has none to whom he can pray any more, since he will be punished anyway. The context in which the question is raised would tend into this direction. Confucius answers here a question of Wangsun Jia, who was a great officer of Wei, and therefore close to the sovereign of Wei. However, as the sentence stands now, it is not stated that it should be limited to the sovereign only. Due to the broader context of the *Analects*, it could apply to the human being in general as well.

---

[16] *Analects* II,4.
[17] Cf. Fu, pp.135, 140; on the possible difference between *tianming* and *ming*, see Hall & Ames, p.211 ff.
[18] *Analects* XVI,8.
[19] *Analects* III,13.

8.3. Conclusion

Taken altogether, one can find no clear statement on Heaven in the *Analects*. The references are too few in number. However, a new aspect does appear. Confucius has a particular and individual relationship with Heaven, and such a relationship is also possible for the superior man. This process of personalisation is accompanied by a greater distance between the human being and Heaven.

Chapter 9: The *Mencius*

9.1. Statistical analysis

> *tian* (天): 78
> *tiandao* (天 道): 1
> *tianming* (天 命): 1
> *tianxia* (天 下): 173
> *tianzi* (天 子): 35
> *mintian* (旻 天): 2
> *shangdi* (上 帝): 3

This statistical analysis shows some relevant characteristics. In comparison with the *Analects*, the references to *tian* are more numerous, though taking into account the size of the work, this should not be overestimated. Moreover, 25 of the references to *tian* appear in three paragraphs (V A,5-7). There are some other parallels with the *Analects*: the high number of references to *tianxia* and *tianzi* indicates how these expressions were used as common words by the time of the compilation of the book. There is only one mention of the term *tianming* (a quotation from the *Book of Odes*[1]), even though *ming* appears as a separate term. Worth noting is also the virtual absence of *tian* with prefix (the two references to *mintian* are supposed to be a citation from the *Book of Documents*[2]). Finally, the references to *shangdi* are extremely reduced in number: two of the three references are quotations from the *Book of Documents*[3] and the *Book of Odes*[4]. *Di* never appears in the sense of High Lord, only in the sense of sovereign. This seems to confirm a trait already present in the *Analects*: the predominance of the term *tian*. As will be seen further, the *Mencius* quotes

---

[1] *Mencius* IV A,8 = ode 235,4.
[2] *Mencius* V A,1; cf. Dayumo (3), p.66
[3] *Mencius* I B,3; cf. Taishi (*shang*) (27), p.286.
[4] *Mencius* IV A,8 = ode 235,4.

relevant materials from the *Book of Documents* and *Book of Odes* heavily. By doing so, it clarifies the historical background and foundation of the idea of Heaven, but adds a new interpretation to it.[5]

9.2. The relationship between Heaven and human beings

One could say that relationship between Heaven and human beings as it appears in the book of *Mencius* follows two tendencies: *tian* has its place in a political theory that follows the line of the *Book of Documents* and the *Book of Odes*; *tian* is also related to a theory about the human being that appeared initially in the *Analects*.

The three actors of the relationship between Heaven and the human being, Heaven, the sovereign and the people as appeared in the *Book of Documents* and the *Book of Odes* can be found in the *Mencius* as well. It is noteworthy that around twelve of the references related to *tian* and *shangdi* are quotations from the *Book of Documents* and the *Book of Odes*, and that nearly all of them describe this relationship of three actors. Generally speaking, *the political idea of Heaven* is consistent with the ideas expressed in these two Classics: the sovereign, who is the minister of Heaven (天 吏)[6], receives the throne of Heaven with a mandate to regulate the people. In I B,3 for instance, Mencius admonishes king Xuan of Qi by quoting two passages from the Classical writing:

"It is said in the *Book of Odes*[7]: 'I fear the Majesty of Heaven, and will thus preserve its favouring decree.' (畏 天 之 威 ， 于 時 保 之) ...
In the *Book of Documents*[8] it is said: 'Heaven having produced the inferior people, made for them rulers and teachers, with the purpose that they should assist the High Lord, and therefore distinguished them throughout the four quarters of the land. (天 降 下 民 ， 作 之 君 ， 作 之 師 ， 惟 曰 其 助 上 帝 ， 寵 之 四 方) Whoever are offenders, and whoever are innocent, here am I [to deal with them]. How dare any under heaven give indulgence to their refractory wills!'"[9]

Still some minor differences, or better shifts in accent, can be found. The growing importance of the role of the people in the Mencian political philosophy, is also reflected in its relation to Heaven (at three instances one even finds the term 天 民)[10]. The *Mencius* not only stresses that Heaven made

---

[5] Cf. Fu (1984), p.152.
[6] *Mencius* II A,5; II B,8.
[7] Ode 272.
[8] Taishi (*shang*) (27), p.286 (slightly different version).
[9] *Mencius* I B,3; see also: II a,4; IV A,1; IV A,8; V A,1; V A,7; VI A,6.
[10] *Mencius* V A,7; V B,1; VII A,19.

124

rulers and teachers "for the people"[11], but also that the people can play a role in the appointment of the sovereign.

The passage of Mencius V A,5 (15 references to *tian*) shows this aspect very clearly. Here Mencius gives his own interpretation of the succession of the sage kings Yao and Shun.[12] They were said to have passed on their throne to an extra lined successor, rather than to their sons, and in this passage the disciple Wan Zhang questions Mencius about this succession. Mencius replies that the transmission of the throne depends not on the ruler's whim, but on Heaven. Wan Zhang responds to this by asking what this means in practical terms: "Does Heaven [transfer to the throne] through explicit decree (*ming*)?" "No", replies Mencius, "Heaven does not speak (天 不 言); it manifests its decree through action and event." Here one can notice Mencius' hesitance to apply the term *ming* to the transmission of the throne, and this might also be one of the explanations for the virtual absence of the term *tianming*. In the description that follows, one can notice the reduced role of Heaven. Mencius explains that before a ruler can pass the throne to a chosen successor, that successor must be approved first by Heaven and second by the people. In the *Book of Documents*, Heaven reacted upon the virtue of a given person, so as to give him a mandate. In the *Mencius*, one can hardly speak of an action by Heaven: Heaven accepts the proposal (天 受 之). Moreover, in the examples given (also in V A,6), the people seem to play a considerable role. Much importance is given to the fact that the people follow the designated successor rather than the son, before Heaven gives him the throne (天 與 之). At the end, it appears that the whole paragraph is an exegesis of the sentence: "Heaven sees through the sight of my people; Heaven hears through the hearing of my people. (天 視 自 我 民 視 ， 天 聽 自 我 民 聽)" from the *Book of Documents*[13]. In the context of the *Book of Documents*, this sentence seems to show that Heaven, in its relationship to the ruler, acts through what it sees and hears from the people. The emphasis is certainly on Heaven. In *Mencius* the role of the people has increased in importance, and less importance is given to Heaven. The will of Heaven became more and more identified with popular consensus.[14] Heaven, as Eno correctly states, disappears in descriptive political realities[15].

However, it is difficult to speak of a consistent theory in the *Mencius*. In one instance, for example, a more active role is given to Heaven:

> "Shun rose from among the channeled fields... Thus, when Heaven is about to confer a great office on any man, it first exercises his mind with suffering, and his sinews and bones with toil. ... By all these

---

[11] *Mencius* I B,3 with quotation of Taishi (*shang*) (27), p.286.
[12] Cf. Eno, pp.104-105.
[13] Taishi (*zhong*) (28), p.292; cf. also Gaoyaomo (8), p.74.
[14] Cf. also Hall and Ames, p.203.
[15] Eno, p.105.

methods it stimulates his mind, hardens his nature, and supplies his incompetencies."[16]

Such a testing of a future sovereign attributed to Heaven was hardly present in the *Book of Documents* or the *Book of Odes*, but it is not the prevalent opinion in the *Mencius* either.

The reduced activity of Heaven can also be observed in its punishing role. This element appears in the *Mencius*, mainly by use of quotations from the *Book of Documents* and the *Book of Odes*, but it is not a dominant element. Reward and punishment become more and more a question of automatic reaction, in which the human being plays a major role. The following passage shows how the *Mencius* selects and interprets citations from the two Classical texts in order to underscore the human responsibility with regard to his obtaining calamity or happiness in this life:

> "Calamity and happiness in all cases are men's own seeking. This is illustrated by what is said in the *Book of Odes*[17]: 'Be always studious to be in harmony with the mandate (永 言 配 命)', so you will certainly get for yourself much happiness.' and by the passage of the *Taijia* [*Book of Documents*][18]: 'When Heaven sends down calamities, it is still possible to escape from them; when we occasion the calamities ourselves, it is not possible any longer to live.' (天 作 孽 ， 猶 可 違 ， 自 作 孽 ， 不 可 活) "[19]

That it is still possible to escape from the calamities sent down by Heaven is certainly not the dominant pattern in the *Book of Documents*, but it is quoted twice in the *Mencius* to illustrate man's responsibility for his action. That Heaven is mainly reduced to an element within a description of political realities also appears in the following passage:

> "When tight government prevails in the kingdom, those of little virtue are submissive to those of great, and those of little worth are submissive to those of great. When bad government prevails in the kingdom, those of small power are submissive to those of great, and the weak to the strong. Both these cases are [the rule of] Heaven. They who accord with Heaven are preserved, and they who rebel against Heaven perish. (順 天 者 存 ， 逆 天 者 亡)"[20]

---

[16] *Mencius* VI B,15.
[17] Ode 235,6; also quoted in *Mencius* IV A,4.
[18] Taijia (*zhong*) (28), p.207; also quoted in *Mencius* IV A,8.
[19] *Mencius* II A,4.
[20] *Mencius* IV A,7.

In this passage, the *Mencius* does not present a theological theory. It is a political theory in which Heaven has its place.

The ruler's response to Heaven also shows a pattern similar to the one in the *Book of Documents*, though with a minor shift. The *Mencius* takes up the idea of "awe" (畏), but at the same time introduces the concept of "delighting in Heaven" (樂 天):

> "He who with a great [state] serves a small one, delights in Heaven. He who with a small [state] serves a large one, stands in awe of Heaven. He who delights in Heaven, will preserve the whole kingdom. He who stands in awe of Heaven, will preserve his own state. It is said in the *Book of Odes*[21]: 'I stand in awe of the majesty of Heaven, and will thus preserve its favouring decree.' (畏 天 之 威 ， 于 時 保 之)"[22]

As can be observed, it is difficult to construct a consistent theory of Heaven from these passages. In Eno's eyes, such an attempt would be to misunderstand their import; the resulting theory would be a shapeless grouping of conflicting ideas. What is intriguing about the passages is precisely that they are governed by no theory of Heaven at all. Heaven had little to contribute to Mencius' political ideas other than to be available as a piece of rhetoric to help Mencius express those ideas however he could.[23]

The second aspect of the concept of Heaven in the *Mencius* is its association with his *theory on man*. This is to a certain extent an elaboration of the *Analects*. The striking difference with the *Analects*, however, is that no particular or unique relationship between Heaven and the person of Mencius is mentioned. There is nothing like Heaven being the source of Mencius mission, using him like a wooden bell, allowing him to be a great Sage or engendering virtue in him. One only finds one descriptive (nearly fatalistic) reference in which Mencius himself is involved: "My not finding [in] the prince of Lu, [a ruler who would confide in me, and put my counsels into practice] is from Heaven (不 遇 魯 侯 ， 天 也)."[24] This absence of a personal decree for Mencius or even of a reference to Confucius' personal decree is rather important. The *Mencius* universalizes this idea of personal decree.[25]

The extended meaning that not only the sovereign, but every cultivated man (*junzi*) has a certain relationship with Heaven is a further

---

[21] Ode 272.
[22] *Mencius* I B,3.
[23] Eno, p.106.
[24] *Mencius* I B,16.
[25] Cf. Fu (1984), p.152.

development of the *Analects*. Of the superior man it is said that "he does not murmur against Heaven, nor grudge against men (君 子 不 怨 天 ，不 尤 人) "[26] (in the *Analects*, Confucius did not murmur against Heaven). There are also three things in which the superior man delights (君 子 有 三 樂), the second of which is: "That when looking up, he has no occasion for shame before Heaven, and below, he has no occasion to blush before men. (仰 不 愧 於 天 ，俯 不 怍 於 人) "[27] Both examples illustrate the attitude the superior man can adopt towards Heaven.

Where the *Mencius* clearly goes beyond the *Analects* is to link Heaven with the human heart (心) and the human nature (性). The beginning of chapter VII, clearly establishes this link:

盡 其 心 者 ，知 其 性 也 ；知 其 性 ，則 知 天 矣 。
存 其 心 ，養 其 性 ，所 以 事 天 也 。殀 壽 不 貳 ，
修 身 以 俟 之 ，所 以 立 命 也 。

To preserve one's heart and to cultivate one's nature is the way to serve Heaven. He who exhausts his heart, knows his nature; to know one's nature is to know Heaven. When neither premature death nor long life causes a man any double-mindedness, but he awaits them while cultivating himself, that is the way in which he establishes his mandate."[28]

Because of the condensed meaning of this sentence, and also because our present interpretation is highly influenced by the Neo-Confucian interpretation, it is difficult to rediscover its original meaning. In terms of relationship, however, one can notice that the subject in these sentences is the human being who is able to "know" (知), "serve" (事) Heaven or "establish" (立) his mandate. Moreover, one can discover in these sentences the foundations of a doctrine of a "personal decree" given to every human being[29]. They not only confirm the personalization of the relationship with Heaven, but open the way to a greater interiorisation.

The interiorisation of the relationship between Heaven and every human being (not only the collective "people") appears more clearly in several passages which reflect a new development in the Mencian anthropological philosophy: the senses of hearing and seeing (耳 目 之 官), and the sense of the heart (心 之 官) which is able to think (思) are said to be

---

[26] *Mencius* II B,13: here also the context goes into a fatalistic direction (compare Eno, p.125).
[27] *Mencius* VII A,20.
[28] *Mencius* VII A,1.
[29] Cf. Eno, p.124 ff.; further developed in VII A,2.

given to the human being by Heaven[30]. Natural abilities (才) are also conferred upon man by Heaven[31]. Yet, where the *Mencius* goes the furthest is to have attributed human virtues to Heaven. This theory is clearly developed in a long passage where Mencius distinguishes between the "nobility of Heaven" (天 爵) and the "nobility of man" (人 爵):

> "Benevolence, righteousness, loyalty and fidelity, unflagging delight in what is good (仁 義 忠 信 樂 善 不 倦): these constitutes the nobility of Heaven. To be a duke, a minister or a counselor: these constitute the nobility of man. The men of antiquity cultivated their nobility of Heaven, and the nobility of man came to them in its train. The men of the present day cultivate their nobility of Heaven in order to seek for the nobility of man, and when they have obtained that, they throw away the other: their delusion is extreme. The issue is simply this, that they must lose [that nobility of man] as well."[32]

To attribute these values to Heaven is certainly a breakthrough in comparison with the *Book of Documents* and the *Book of Odes*, but also in comparison with the *Analects*. This indicates a further interiorisation of the concept of Heaven. One can also observe the role of the human being as underlined in this paragraph: the human being is supposed to cultivate (修) the nobility of Heaven. One can also add that in Mencius' eyes, among these virtues, benevolence (仁) was "the most honorable nobility conferred by Heaven, and the quiet home in which man should dwell"[33]. Finally, also the virtue of sincerity (誠) is connected to Heaven, even if there is only a short reference to it: "Sincerity is the way of Heaven. To think [how to] be sincere is the way of man." (誠 者 ， 天 之 道 也 ， 思 誠 者 ， 人 之 道 也)[34]

9.3. Conclusion

It is difficult to find a consistent theory of Heaven in the *Mencius*. In general, it has its place in the Mencian political theory in which the role of the people is increased, and in which the reaction of Heaven becomes more automatic. With regard to the significance of Heaven in Mencius' anthropology, it not only becomes more universal and personalized but also more interiorised.

---

[30] *Mencius* VI A,15.
[31] *Mencius* VI A,7.
[32] *Mencius* VI A,16.
[33] *Mencius* II A,7.
[34] *Mencius* IV A,13

Chapter 10: The Classics and the *Ditiankao*

In the second part of this dissertation we tried to analyse the relationship between Heaven and the human being as it appears in the *Book of Documents*, the *Book of Odes*, the *Analects* and the *Mencius*. We focused on questions like "Who is in contact with Heaven" and "What type of relationship is it?". By focusing our research on the question of relationship, we quite consciously did not raise the questions of anthropomorphism, transcendence, immanence etc. which have been discussed previously by many authors.

As a conclusion of this part we would like to situate the results of this research within a broader horizon by confronting them with the studies done by Rudolf Otto and Mircea Eliade. We will also take up the *Ditiankao* where we have left it earlier, and compare the text with the results of this second part.

10.1. The Chinese sky god

In his study on the *Idea of the Holy*[1], Rudolf Otto distinguishes between the two notions of *mysterium tremendum* and *mysterium fascinosum*. Conceptually, he says, *mysterium* (something wholly other than ourselves) denotes merely that which is hidden and esoteric, that which is beyond conception or understanding, extraordinary and unfamiliar. The term does not define the object positively in its qualitative character. Although what is enunciated in the word is negative, what is meant is something absolutely and intensely positive. Moreover, we can experience this pure positive by the feelings it arouses in our hearts.

The feelings that the human being experiences in response to the holy, are divided by Otto into *tremendum* and *fascinosum*. *Tremor* is in itself

---

[1] Cf. Otto, chap.4: "Mysterium Tremendum".

131

merely the perfectly familiar and 'natural' emotion of fear. But the term as understood by Otto, denotes a quite specific kind of emotional response, wholly distinct from that of being afraid. In English it is best rendered by the term "awe": it implies an "absolute inapproachability". A further element added to the *tremendum* is that of might, power, "absolute overpoweringness" represented by the term of *majestas* (majesty). At the same time, however, the mysterious has another aspect, in which it shows itself as something uniquely *fascinating*. Here the human being is intensely attracted and dynamically impelled towards the Other. The experiences which belong to the *fascinosum* are love, mercy, pity, and comfort.

If one confronts our analysis with these concepts, one easily comes to the conclusion that the *tremendum* is the dominant characteristic of the deities in the works we have analysed. This is particularly true for the *Book of Documents*. Heaven is distant from the people and only communicates with the sovereign through "mandates", not through personal or affective communication; Heaven is reactive rather than active; Heaven, though bright, inspires "fear and awe". The *Book of Odes* not only presents a similar awe filled concept of Heaven, but that idea is even enforced in the poems of lamentations: Heaven is terrifying, unjust and blind. The *Analects* contain a new dimension. In the person of Confucius, Heaven and the human being seem closer to each other. Still, it is difficult to speak of a fascinating Heaven. The punishing and terrifying Heaven remains predominant, and the calls for the superior man to stand in awe of the Decree of Heaven underlines this aspect. Finally, in the *Mencius*, Heaven does not speak and remains passive. Only the "delight" one can take in Heaven, and the link that is made by Mencius between Heaven and the human heart indicates the possibility of fascination, but the attitude of awe is not reduced.

The analysis Mircea Eliade has made of the "sky and sky gods"[2] throws an additional light on these deities. We join Mircea Eliade in categorizing *tian* as a "sky god". Mircea Eliade insists on the fact that before looking at the divine figures of the sky, one has to grasp the religious significance of the sky as such. Even before any religious values have been set upon the sky it reveals its transcendence. The sky "symbolizes" transcendence, power and changelessness simply by being there. It exists because it is high, infinite, immovable, powerful. The mere fact of being high, of being high up, means being powerful (in religious sense), and as such being filled with the sacred. The symbolism of its transcendence derives from the simple realization of its infinite height. "Most high" becomes quite naturally an attribute of the divinity. According to Eliade's analysis it is difficult to say precisely when the hierophany of the sky became personified, when the divinities of the sky showed themselves, or took the place of the holiness of the sky as such. What is quite certain is that the sky divinities have always been supreme divinities; that their hierophanies have remained for

---

[2] Eliade, chap.2: "Sky and sky gods", esp. pp.38-40; see also Eliade (1987).

that reason sky hierophanies; and that what one may call the history of the divinities is largely a history of notions of "force", of "creation", of "laws" and of "sovereignty".

Much of what Eliade wrote can be applied to the deities that we found in the four works we analysed.[3] As far as the name of these deities is concerned, the character *tian* means "sky", though the original meaning might be "great". The other name used to underline its sovereignty is *di* or Lord, to which the prefix *shang* ("High") was added. One also finds the expression *shangtian* ("High Heaven"). The other prefixes like *huang, hao* and the most complete combination *huangtian shangdi* all indicate the supremacy of the Chinese sky god. As regard to their manifestation, we have been less concerned with the history of the fusion between *shangdi* and *tian*. In general they are interchangeable, even if we pointed out some differences between the two terms, especially in the *Book of Documents* and the *Book of Odes*. This also appears in their hierophanies, which all tend in the direction of the sovereignty of a sky god. They are revealed as a hierophany of cosmic rhythm and order. It is the sky that regulates the order of the cosmos. The sky is a dynastic providence, an all-seeing and law-giving power. The Chinese sky god also shares another specific trait of sky gods, passivity. Passivity was already present in the reactive attitude of Heaven in the *Book of Documents*, but it became more apparent in the *Mencius*.

One can also compare the "history" of the Chinese sky god with the "history" of other sky gods. One can discern a phenomenon which is extremely significant in the religious history of mankind in the "history" of Supreme Beings and sky gods. These divine figures tend to disappear from the cult. This is what Eliade calls the phenomenon of the *deus otiosus* or the god at leisure.[4] Nowhere do they play a leading part, but have become remote and are replaced by other religious forces, such as ancestor-worship and worship of the spirits and the gods of nature.

The Chinese sky god seems to be an exception to this evolution. Eliade himself noticed that a few sky gods preserved their position in people's religious life, or even strengthened it, by being seen as sovereign gods as well[5]. There are those who were best able to maintain their supremacy in the pantheon, among which Eliade classifies *tian*, and those who were subject of monotheistic revolutions (e.g. YHWH). It is true that *tian* has maintained its supremacy throughout Chinese history. It was seen as the highest divinity responsible for the cosmic and dynastic order. But the Chinese sky god also shares some characteristics of the *deus otiosus*. This is due to the original hierarchy of heaven - sovereign - people. The distance between heaven and the people has been vast. Later in history this distance was preserved and even increased since, besides ancestor worship, the people

---

[3] See also Eliade, pp.62-63, p.94 (with reference to Granet); cf. Granet, p.64 ff.
[4] Eliade, p.46 ff.; p.109.
[5] Eliade, pp.110-111.

could address prayers to a whole series of intermediate gods and goddesses (also Buddhist and Taoist ones). Heaven did not disappear, it was there, but remote, passive, and distant. Only the sovereign kept his direct and individual relationship with Heaven through the (annual) sacrifices. The people did not enter into direct communication with Heaven, and if they did (such as in some Taoist ceremonies) it always seems to be as a collective body. The writings we have studied have shown some aspects of this evolution. In the *Book of Documents* and the *Book of Odes*, it is not too difficult to interpret *shangdi* or *tian* as an anthropomorphic being. This becomes much more difficult in the *Analects* and in the *Mencius* where *shangdi* (the most anthropomorphic concept of the two) tends to disappear.

The *Analects* and the *Mencius*, however, also present a view where Heaven and the human being seem to come closer to each other. This is certainly true for the process of personification in which the decree of Heaven becomes a personal decree. However, this process of personification and even interiorisation is accompanied in most cases by a further distance. Heaven becomes more and more "Nature" or "Fate". Heaven does not speak, and in the individual's response all cult is absent (there are no sacrifices of the individual to Heaven). As occasionally happened with other sky gods, the ubiquity, the wisdom and the passivity of the Chinese sky god were seen afresh in a metaphysical sense, and the god became the epiphany of the order of nature and the moral law; the divine "person" gave place to the "idea"; religious experience (already meager in the case of almost all the sky gods) gave place to theoretic understanding, or philosophy[6]. This tendency appears in the *Analects* and in the *Mencius*, and was later fully developed by the Song commentaries on these writings, as we have seen in Zhu Xi's identification of *tian* with *li* (principle).

10.2. A powerful God

It seems appropriate at this stage to make a short comparison between the analysis we made in the second part of this dissertation and the *Ditiankao* of Yan Mo. It would be unfair, however, to evaluate Yan Mo's writing on the basis of the present analysis. Not only would it be unfair because one cannot simply project a 20th century research on a 17th century text, written in quite a different context. But also because the present research does not have the pretension to have presented a complete view on *Tian* and *Shangdi* in these classical works. As stated before, we only followed one line, which should be complemented by other analyses such as those of Fu, Eno or Tien. Still, we will attempt a short comparison so as to appreciate the specificity of Yan Mo's text more.

---

[6] Eliade, p.110.

A first striking element is that the majority of the quotations cited by Yan Mo are taken from the *Book of Documents* (33 quotations) and the *Book of Odes* (26 quotations), whereas there are but a small number taken from the *Four Books* (the *Analects*: 2; the *Doctrine of the Mean*: 1; the *Mencius*: 3). This has quite a important influence on the idea of God as presented in his analysis. Indeed, the idea of a more personal anthropomorphic deity in the *Book of Documents* and in the *Book of Odes* corresponds better to the Christian God as presented by the missionaries. The *Analects* or the *Mencius* propose a more distant Heaven, which can be more easily interpreted as Fate or Nature. Moreover, the concept of *tian* in these two writings was subjected much more to the interpretation by the Song authors, like Zhu Xi, who were explicitly rejected by Yan Mo.

The global impression of the God presented in Yan Mo's writing is that of a powerful God: great, august, vast, omnipotent, omnipresent, rewarding the good and punishing the bad. The human reaction is one of standing in awe, being careful and reverent, being aware that those who follow God become saints and sages, and that those who go against him become mean people. It is obvious that the dominant aspect is *tremendum*. This should not surprise us. It not only corresponds quite well to the predominant image of Heaven and High Lord in the *Book of Documents* and the *Book of Odes*, but it also corresponds to a large extent to the image of God as presented by the missionaries. Moreover, it is also influenced by the term controversy in reaction to which it was written. Yan Mo had to show the superiority of *Shangdi* and *Tian*, in order to prove that these concepts were equal to the supreme God *Tianzhu*.

Yet it would be wrong to qualify Yan Mo's God merely as *tremendum*, since there are also clear examples of the *fascinosum* aspect. Yan Mo also speaks of Heaven as "sheltering and aiding" (陰 相), "compassionating" (矜), "speaking" (謂), etc. all qualifications which only have a minor place in the *Book of Documents* and the *Book of Odes*. He also gives God the attributes of "supreme living" (至 活) and "supreme benevolent" (至 仁), which cannot be found in these writings. On the side of the human being, he adopts Mencius' concept of "delighting in Heaven" (樂 天) as well.

There is another aspect where Heaven and the human being come closer to each other in Yan Mo's writing. We have seen that in section 2b of his *Personal Discussion* Yan Mo describes the historical experience of the relationship between Heaven and the human being. Many of his examples refer to a political context in which we find the three actors Heaven, sovereign and the people that were present in the Classical writings. But Yan Mo does not limit the sages and saints to kings and sovereigns, since in his text all people are called to follow the appointment given to them by Heaven. We have so to say a Mencian reading of the quotations from the *Book of*

Documents and *Book of Odes*[7]. However, in the *Mencius* we have seen that on the one hand the concept of personal decree resulted in an interiorisation, while on the other hand it resulted in a greater distance between Heaven and man. In Yan Mo's text we find a few traces of this interiorisation: the High Lord has given birth to the human being and endowed it with nature, with a moral sense, with things and rules, with a spiritual nature (soul). More important, however, is that Yan Mo gives an extended meaning to sentences with a political character as well (the history of saints and sages). All people are called to follow the appointment given to them by Heaven in all their walkings and doings. Every human being is called to serve God. Unlike the *Analects* or the *Mencius*, this does not result in a greater distance between Heaven and the human being.

In this context it is interesting to look closer at the selection of quotations Yan Mo has taken from the *Analects* and the *Mencius*. A sentence like "He who offends against Heaven has none to whom he can pray"[8] is clearly given a more universal meaning, as is the other sentence from the *Analects*: "The superior man stands in awe of the decree of Heaven. The mean man does not know the decree of Heaven and [consequently] does not stand in awe of it."[9] From the *Mencius*, Yan Mo selects the two opening sentences of chapter VII A. In the second (which is the only sentence in the *Ditiankao* without reference to *tian* or *shangdi*) it is said that "there is a decree for everything; obey by receiving [those commands] proper [to you]. (莫 非 命 也 ， 順 受 其 正)"[10] Again, as it appears here, the sentence is not limited to the sovereign. Finally Yan Mo quotes also the very dubious sentence: "Though a man may be wicked, yet if he adjusts his thoughts, fasts and cleanses himself, he would be fit to offer sacrifices to the High Lord. (雖 有 惡 人 ， 齊 戒 沐 浴 則 可 以 祀 上 帝)"[11] This sentence is dubious because traditionally the sacrifice to the High Lord was reserved for the king alone. Yan Mo adopts Zhu Xi's commentary that this sentence encourages man to renew himself (自 新). In fact, for all these sentences Yan Mo adopts the interpretation of the Song commentary which extended the meaning of these phrases to every superior man. The difference, however, is that Yan Mo rejects the more distant and natural concept of *tian* given by these commentaries, and interprets them in terms of a more personal God.

Here the concepts of Eliade are of some help. We have seen that the history of the Chinese sky god underwent a process similar to other sky gods, namely becoming to a certain extent a *deus otiosus*. Yan Mo is aware of this process, though not in explicit terms. We have already pointed out several

---

[7] The last two sentences of section 2a are a paraphrase of *Mencius* followed by quotations from the *Book of Documents* and the *Book of Odes*. The end of the whole section 2b has two quotations from the *Mencius*.
[8] [60] = *Analects* III,13.
[9] [61] = *Analects* XVI,8; the second part only in version B.
[10] [64] = *Mencius* VII A,2.
[11] [65] = *Mencius* IV B,24.

136

times his rejection of the Song interpretation of the concepts of *tian* and *shangdi*. By going back to the concept of a sky god from before the process of *deus otiosus*, Yan Mo also goes back to the characteristics of the original sky god: high, infinite, immovable, powerful.

As can be observed, Yan Mo did not simply give a Christian meaning to the Chinese Classics. The encounter with the Western God gave him the opportunity to start a creative dialogue with his own tradition. Moreover, this dialogue, both traditional and new, resulted in a new interpretation of the Chinese concept of Heaven.

Conclusion: The Fascinating God

In the present dissertation we have taken a long *detour*. First we studied the view of a Chinese lay theologian who tried to prove that the Chinese concepts of *Shangdi* and *Tian* were equal to the Western *Tianzhu*. In order to better appreciate his thought, we went even further back in history and analysed the four major writings on which he based his argument. At the end of this process we would like to make some comments which might be of some help for present-day theological reflection.

At first we would like to point out some similarities and differences between the concepts of *Shangdi* and *Tian* and the Christian God as they appear from these writings. We will conclude with a reflection on the word for God itself.

11.1. Similarities

The *Ditiankao* and the analysis of the *Book of Documents*, the *Book of Odes*, the *Analects* and the *Mencius* have pointed out quite a number of similarities.

These similarities are in the first place due to *experience*. The classical writings, among other things, reflect the experience of transcendence by a people or by individuals. This experience was given a name, *Shangdi* and/or *Tian*, and was incorporated into a political theology. According to these writings, in the Shang and Zhou dynasty, the Chinese people experienced that human government was not sufficient by itself. It was related to a higher force, a sky god, who was supreme, powerful, rewarding and punishing. Later this sky god was also seen as the origin of human nature and human values. The author of the *Ditiankao*, Yan Mo, belongs to the tradition which has gone through this experience, even if this experience received another interpretation in the Song dynasty. But the fact that he himself belongs to a Chinese (mainly Confucian) tradition which had at least

139

a certain experience of what was given the name *Shangdi* or *Tian* in origin is important. Another facet is added to his belonging to a Chinese tradition, that of belonging to a Christian tradition. One can certainly speak of a tradition. Yan Mo not only identified with the Christian faith as presented by a mainly Thomistic theology, he also refers to the historical development of that faith, and the ancient scriptures of the West. Finally, one may suppose that Yan Mo had a personal experience of God (although we have no explicit reference to it), and that this transcendental experience encouraged him to take a clear position against those who declared that the *Shangdi* and *Tian* in whom he believed were not the same as the *Tianzhu* in whom he believed.

It is this triple experience, of belonging to a Chinese tradition which had an experience of *Shangdi* and *Tian*, of belonging to a Christian tradition which had an experience of *Tianzhu*, and of his personal experience of God, that enabled him to identify these realities and to create a new interpretation of the Chinese Classics as written down in the *Ditiankao*.

In this process of reinterpretation, elements of both the Christian and the Confucian tradition were present. Like many other Chinese Christians, he was a convinced Confucian and remained so after his conversion. But to him conversion meant that a new dimension was added to his Confucian faith. In effect, this meant that certain canonical key passages acquired a new significance.[1] It is noteworthy that this new significance is in many respects closer to the present-day interpretation of these texts than the Song commentaries.

Yan Mo's analysis focused on the similarities. The obvious reason is that he believed that the God as presented by the Thomistic theology of the missionaries was indeed in many aspects similar to the deities *Shangdi* and *Tian* as can be found mainly in the *Book of Documents* and the *Book of Odes*. Another reason for the prevalence of similarities is the historical context of the text. It is a apologetic text which consciously wanted to prove that these terms were similar, against those who stated that they were not.

Without doubt, by stressing these similarities, the text gives the impression of going in the direction of *Tianzhu*-ism. The term *Tianzhu*-ism was recently coined by E. Zürcher to underline that writings of Chinese Christians focus on *Tianzhu*, while the person of Jesus Christ and the whole question of incarnation is given relatively little attention.[2] It would be wrong to say, as Zürcher makes clear, that incarnation is given no attention in their writings. However, this problem of Christian doctrine is marginalised, since the emphasis is not upon redemption but upon the Lord of Heaven as an omnipotent creator and a stern judge. This is certainly true for Yan Mo's text which we analysed. There are a few minor references to the Trinity,

---

[1] Cf. Zürcher, pp.2-3.
[2] Zürcher, p.20.

incarnation and the Son who was given birth by the Father. Full attention, however, is given to the powerful *Tianzhu*. One should add that this *Tianzhu*-ism was not only due to the fact that Chinese (converts) could more easily accept the notion of God than the notion of Christ. Furthermore, because the term-controversy focused on the notion of God, it largely contributed to *Tianzhu*-ism as well.

11.2. Differences

It is at this point that we can proceed to the question of the differences. It is not our purpose to make an exhaustive list of all possible differences between the Christian God and the Chinese *Shangdi* and *Tian*. Recent studies have amply shown these differences[3]. We only select a few aspects. We will remain faithful to the analysis we made and therefore continue to focus on the relationship between Heaven and the human being. How can the confrontation with Yan Mo's text deepen this analysis?

In the analysis of the Classical writings, we have paid much attention to the triple relationship between Heaven, the sovereign and the people, and we have seen that this relationship underwent some evolution (through interiorisation). An important element, however, is that generally speaking this relationship has been maintained throughout all of Chinese history: the sovereign was the only individual to address himself in a very specific and direct way to Heaven. For the people this relationship remained collective: Heaven was present but distant. Individuals had hardly any direct relationship with Heaven, they had a direct relationship with other gods or divinities. In the case of interiorisation, as seen in the *Analects* and *Mencius*, and later also developed by the Song commentators, one can hardly speak of a direct relationship, since the individual would not address the *deus otiosus*, nor would he sacrifice to him. It is within this context that introduction of *Tianzhu* becomes significant.

Let us first notice that in the Christian scriptures one can also find examples of a triple relationship between God, an individual and the people. The whole story of the exodus (in *Exodus* and *Deuteronomy*) is such an example: Moses is the individual who acts as an intermediary between the people (spoken of as a collective body) and God, with whom only Moses enters into direct dialogue. This episode certainly shows a number of similarities with the traditional Chinese view of relationship between Heaven and human being.[4] Therefore it should not surprise us that "Moses'

---

[3] Cf. Fang Chih-jung; Fang, comparing the results of Lo Kuang's research with his own research in biblical exegesis points out such differences as God considered as Father, God as Love, God saving his people, etc.

[4] There are also some differences: God is much more active and dialogues with Moses (Heaven does not dialogue with the sovereign); moreover, the commands of God are given to the people; in some of the preaching of the Early Church, such as Paul's preaching before the Jews

Admonishment of the People" is taken by another Chinese student of theology, Wu Li S.J. 吳 歷 (1732-1718) as a model for a set of poems. These can be easily read as an admonishment of the Chinese people as well.[5]

Yet, the God introduced by Christianity in China is a God who not only has a collective relationship with the people, but who has an individual relationship with every individual human being as well. In the creation myths, the stories of life and death, or the conversion stories of the Christian scriptures we find kings and commoners, rich and poor, men and women alike who enter into an individual relationship with God. This relationship is as individual as the one *Shangdi* and *Tian* had with the sovereign in the Chinese tradition. In Yan Mo's writing we have clearly seen how the quotations from the Classics were interpreted in this sense. It is important to realize that this is in itself a radical change in the Classical Chinese theology. This new relationship between Heaven and the human being, introduces not only a new vision of a personal Heaven, a Master of Heaven, but also a new vision of the human being: the birth of the individual. Certainly Classical Chinese thought did not lack the idea of the individual, but this analysis hopes to have shown that the new concept of God gives birth to a new human being: the individual who no longer needs the sovereign or the collective body: he or she can address him or herself directly to a God who has a personal relationship with this human being.[6]

Accompanying this evolution, one can observe another difference. We have seen that the predominant characteristic of the Chinese sky god was the *tremendum* aspect. We have noticed that in Yan Mo's text, *tremendum* was also largely present, but there was some mention of *fascinosum*. Herein lies a further difference between *Shangdi*, *Tian* and the Christian God. This difference was already noticed by Chief Grand Secretary Ye Xianggao in the quotation that appears at the beginning of this book. In his eyes, Chinese scholars speak about Heaven as something high and distant, whereas the Westerners speak about Heaven as something close, affectionate and intimate. This difference is probably even more apparent in present-day theology than in the Thomistic theology. We have noticed in the introduction that a major evolution in Catholic theology in the 20th century was the rediscovery of the scriptures. If one limits oneself to the Old Testament[7], one can find many aspects of *tremendum*: the wrath of God, the punishing God, God as judge, the God of war, etc., together with the corresponding human

---

in *Acts* 13,17 ff. one finds the triple relationship between God, the king and the people: Jesus Christ has finally taken the place of the king.

[5] *Meise yuzhong yuezhang* 每 瑟 諭 衆 樂 章 in Fang Hao (1969), pp.1638-1642; see also Chaves, pp.78-79.

[6] In the early Chinese Church, the celebration of Eucharist was felt as an offense to the mediating function of the Sovereign who alone was allowed to offer sacrifices to Heaven. Even to day Chinese culture does not easily accept such a direct relationship. The Chinese State always tries to intervene as a mediator.

[7] Cf. Chang Ch'un-shen on God in the New Testament, see e.g. Rahner (1961).

reaction of fear and awe. But the fascinating aspect is prevalent as well: the loving and caring God, God in search of the human being, entering into dialogue with individuals, taking care of widows and poor, always ready for forgiveness, ... and the corresponding human reaction of seeking, praising, singing, loving, dancing for God. In addition, modern theology has emphasized these aspects[8]: the Christian God is a self-communicating God, God suffers with the people, God shares both male and female human characteristics,... The Christian God is indeed much more *fascinosum* than what we know of *Shangdi* and *Tian*. By focusing on the similarities, Yan Mo's text was not able to sufficiently show this characteristic. However, his text has helped us to discover the challenge which the fascinating God presents to modern Chinese theology.

A final difference is that the Christian sky god underwent an evolution that was quite different from the other sky gods. We have noticed that the Chinese sky god, similar to the Christian one, maintained its superiority but in many respects retired as well (*deus otiosus*). The Christian sky god, not only maintained its superiority, but has become even more present through incarnation. We have seen that to a certain extent Yan Mo has reversed the Chinese tradition; he rejects the process of *deus otiosus* and interprets the *Analects* and the *Mencius* with the theology of the *Book of Documents* and the *Book of Odes*. As such he comes closer to the Christian concept of God as well. But present-day theology would underline even more the Christian faith of a sky god becoming man, in a very specific place, at a very determinate time in history, speaking the language of one people, using the local customs, living together with ordinary people, but also being condemned and killed and finally resurrected. The faith in a "Western" sky god who shares many characteristics of the Chinese sky god, might not be so difficult for a Chinese. But the faith in a sky god who became man in a foreign country without any record of it in Chinese source is really problematic for a Chinese person (as it is finally for any Christian believer).

11.3. The word for God

It is at this point that we can finalize our dissertation with a reflection on the word for God itself. At the end of this analysis one might expect that the author makes a choice between the different names for God in Chinese, either *Shangdi*, *Tian* or *Tianzhu*. Yan Mo himself expressed his preference for the word *Shangdi*, but he continued to use the other words. Such a choice, however, would require further study of the history both of the Chinese terms and of the Hebrew and Greek terms used in the Bible. Besides prudence should be adopted by someone who does not belong to the Chinese tradition in making a choice for one or another concept. One should not forget, as Rahner has pointed out, that it would be an extremely obscure

---

[8] See e.g. Rahner (1978), see also Schoonenberg, ch.III.3.

and difficult question to ask how we could know that the same thing or the same person is meant by these different words, because in each of these cases we cannot simply point to a common experience of what is meant independently of the word itself.[9]

While admitting the necessity to make a choice (such as for the translation of the Bible), we would like to challenge the three concepts we analysed, by confronting them with what Rahner says about the German word *Gott*.[10] This word, Rahner points out, says nothing or nothing more than that *about* God. Whether this was always the case in the earliest history of the word is another question. In any case the word "God" functions today like a proper name. One has to know from other sources what or who it means. Usually we do not notice this, but it is true. If we were to call God "Father", for example, or "Lord", or the "heavenly being", or something similar [cf."High Lord" (上 帝), "Heaven" (天), "Master of Heaven" (天 主)], as happens all the time in the history of religion, then the word by itself would say something about what it means because of its origins in other experiences we have and in its secular usage. But here it looks in the first instance as though the word confronts us like a blank face. It says nothing about what it means. Nevertheless, Rahner goes on, it is obviously quite appropriate for what it refers to: the "ineffable one", the "nameless one" who does not enter into the world we can name as a part of it. It means the "silent one" who is always there, and yet can always be overlooked, unheard, the one who, because it expresses the whole in its unity and totality, can be passed over as meaningless. It means that which really is wordless, because every word receives its limits, its own sound and hence its intelligible sense only within a field of words. Hence what has become faceless, that is, the word "God" which no longer refers by itself to a definite, individual experience, has assumed the right form to be able to speak to us of God. For it is the final word before we become silent, the word which allows all the individual things we can name to disappear into the background, the word in which we are dealing with the totality which grounds them all.

Reading this meditation of Rahner on the word "God", one can at least ask whether the notions we have analysed are able to function in the same way, namely to bring the human being face to face with the single whole of reality, with the single whole of its own existence. Maybe some other Chinese concepts, such as Dao (道), fulfill this role better.

Facing inadequacy of these notions to express the idea of God, one is confronted with two solutions which can be employed simultaneously. Since no notion can exhaust the reality of God, one will always have to use of a multiplicity of words. Each of these words will express one or more aspects

---

[9] This is not only true for a comparison between the Christian God and *Shangdi* or *Tian*, but also for a comparison between *Shangdi* (deity of the Shang) and *Tian* (deity of the Zhou).
[10] Rahner (1978), p.45 ff.

of God's reality. The other solution is to use whatever term in a prudent, i.e. indirect approach. Rahner, both in speaking and in writing applied this method to the German word *Gott* itself, implicitly recognizing the inadequacy of even that word. He used to say "that which - or better him whom - we call God"[11]. Maybe this is a good way to express the *fascinosum* in a *tremendum* way, even in Chinese.

---

[11] E.g. Rahner (1974), p.159; Rahner most often used the expression "das was wir 'Gott' nennen".

11.4. Conclusion in the form of short theses

1) Since the writings of 17th century Chinese lay theologians are in one way or another seeking an answer to the question: "How to express the Christian faith and experience when entering Chinese culture?", a dialogue with their writings can be fruitful for an inculturated theology today.

2) Any reflection on the notion of God in the Chinese language is the result of a triple experience: the Chinese tradition which had an experience of God; the Christian tradition with its experience; and a personal experience of God.

3) By quoting Classical Chinese texts to prove that the notions of *Shangdi* and *Tian* are the same as the Christian *Tianzhu*, Yan Mo not only gave a new interpretation to these Classical texts, he also put the notion of the Christian God into a new perspective.

4) Besides the many similarities with the traditional Chinese concept of Heaven, the Christian God as brought by the missionaries also introduced some significant differences in this tradition: the Christian God is in many respects a fascinating God, who comes close to the human being, and who enters into a personal relationship with each individual being.

5) Any word for God is inadequate: this inadequacy can be supplemented by the use of multiple terms, but also by a prudent, indirect and reverent use of every term chosen.

Bibliography

Note on the references to literature used

1. Yan Mo's writings (*Caogao, Cunpupian, Ditiankao, Jizukao, Shishu bian cuojie*, etc.) are not included in the bibliography since a detailed description can be found in the section "Yan Mo's writings" of chapter 1.

2. For Ricci's *Tianzhu shiyi*, page reference is given to the Wu Xiangxiang's photoreproduction (see bibliography); the number between brackets that is added refers to the paragraph number in Lancashire's translation.

3. For the *Book of Documents*, reference is given to the name of the chapter, the number of the chapter (according to Legge's *Chinese Classics*: see Table at the beginning of chapter 6), and the page number in Legge's *Chinese Classics* (although the translation is not necessarily his). An underlined chapter number indicates that it is an Old Text chapter.

4. For the *Book of Odes*, reference is given to the number of the Ode according to Kalgren's *The Book of Odes*; in the translation of the *List of Quotations* (chapter 3), the page number of Legge's *Chinese Classics* is added between brackets.

List of quoted writings

Allan, Sarah, *The Shape of the Turtle: Myth, Art and Cosmos in Early China*, New York (SUNY), 1991.

Apologie des Domincains, Cologne, 1699.

Bernard, H., "Les adaptations chinoises d'ouvrages européens: bibliographie chronologique", *Monumenta Serica* 10 (1945), pp.1-57, 307-388.

Biermann, B.M., *Die Anfänge der neueren Dominikanermission in China*, Münster, 1927.

Chan, Wing-tsit, "Chu Hsi on T'ien", in W.T.Chan, *Chu Hsi: New Studies*, Honolulu (University of Hawaii Press), 1989, pp.184-196.

Chang Ch'un-shen Aloysius 張 春 申, "Jiuyue de tianzhuguan" 舊 約 的 天 主 觀 (God in the Old Testament), *Collectanea Theologica Universitatis Fujen* 62 (1984), pp.593-611.

Chaves, Jonathan, *Singing of the Source: Nature and God in the Poetry of the Chinese Painter Wu Li*, Honolulu (Univ. of Hawaii Press), 1993.

Chen Xiyong 陳 錫 勇, *Zongfa tianming yu chunqiu sixiang chutan* 宗 法 天 命 與 春 秋 思 想 初 探 [Primary Investigation into the Mandate of Heaven in the Patriarchal Clan System and the Thought of the Spring and Autumn Period], Taibei (Wenjin chubanshe), 1992.

Chen Yuan 陳 垣, *Chen Yuan xueshu lunwenji* 陳 垣 學 術 論 文 集 [Collected Scholarly Writings by Chen Yuan], Beijing, 1980.

Colombel, Aug. M., *Histoire de la Mission du Kiang-nan: Deuxième Partie: 1644-1840*, Ms., n.p., n.d.

Compagnon, A., *La seconde main ou le travail de la citation*, Paris, 1979.

Courant, M., *Catalogue des Livres Chinois, Coréens, Japonais, etc.*, Paris, 1912.

Creel, Herrlee G., "Appendix C: The Origin of the Diety T'ien", in *The Origins of Statecraft in China: vol.I: The Western Chou Empire*, Chicago/London (The University of Chicago Press), 1970, pp.493-506.

Dehergne, Joseph, "Les chrétientés de Chine de la période Ming (1581-1650)", *Monumenta Serica* 16 (1957), pp.1-136.

Dehergne, Joseph, "La Chine Centrale vers 1700: II Les vicariats apostoliques de la côte (Etude de géographie missionnaire)", *Archivum Historicum Societatis Iesu* XXX (1961), pp.307-366.

Dehergne, Joseph, *Répertoire des Jésuites de Chine de 1552 à 1800*, Rome/Paris, 1973.

Dudink, A., "The Rediscovery of a Seventeenth-Century Collection of Chinese Christian Texts: The Manuscript *Tianxue jijie*", *Sino-Western Cultural Relations Journal* XV (1993), pp.1-26.

Eliade, Mircea, *Patterns in Comparative Religion*, (transl.) R. Sheed, New York (Meridian), 1963.

Eliade, Mircea & Laurence E. Sullivan, "Deus Otiosus", in. M.Eliade, *The Encyclopedia of Religion*, New York, Macmillan, 1987, vol.4, pp.314-318.

Elman, Benjamin A., *From Philosophy to Philology: Intellectual and Social Aspects in Late Imperial China*, Cambridge (Mass.) (Harvard Univ. Press), 1984.

Eno, Robert, "Masters of the Dance: The Role of T'ien (Heaven) in the Teachings of the Early Juist Community", Ann Arbor, Ph.D. Diss. University of Michigan, 1984.

Eno, Robert, *The Confucian Creation of Heaven: Philosophy and the Defense of Ritual Mastery*, Albany (State University of New York Press), 1990. (1990a)

Eno, Robert, "Was There a High God *Ti* in Shang Religion?", *Early China* 15 (1990), pp.1-26. (1990b)

Fang Chih-jung, Mark 房志榮, "Rujia zhi tian yu shengjing de shangdi" 儒家之天與聖經的上帝 (Heaven and the Biblical Notion of God), *Collectanea Theologica Universitatis Fujen* 31 (1977), pp.15-41.

Fang Hao 方豪, "Yingyin *Tiandikao* xu" 影印天帝考序 [Preface to the photoreproduction of the *Tiandikao*], in Wu Xiangxiang 吳相湘 (ed.), *Zhongguo shixue congshu* 中國史學叢書 [Collection on Chinese History], no.40: *Tianzhujiao dongchuan wenxian xubian* 天主教東傳文獻續編 [Second Collection of Documents on the Spread of Catholicism in the East], Taibei, 1966, vol.1, pp.7-9.

Fang Hao 方豪, *Fang Hao liushi zidinggao* 方豪六十自定稿 (The Collected Works of Maurus Fang Hao, Revised and Edited by the Author in his Sixtieth Birthday), 2 vols., Taibei, 1969.

Fang Hao 方豪, "Yan Mo" 嚴謨 [Yan Mo], in *Zhongguo Tianzhujiao renwuzhuan* 中國天主教人物傳 [Biographies of Famous Chinese Catholics], vol. 2, Hong Kong/ Taizhong, 1970.

Feng, Youlan (Fung, Yu-lan), *A History of Chinese Philosophy: vol.1: The Period of the Philosphers*, (transl.Derk Bodde), Princeton (Princeton Univ. Press), 1952.

Feng Youlan 馮友蘭, *Zhongguo zhexueshi xinbian* 中國哲學史新編 [New Edition of the History of Chinese Philosophy], Beijing (People's Publishing House), 1982, vol.1.

Finazzo, Giancarlo, *The Principle of Tien* 天 : *Essay on its Theoretical Relevancy in Early Confucian Philosophy*, Taibei (Mei Ya Publications), 1967.

Fu, Pei-jung, "The Concept of *T'ien* in Ancient China: With Special Emphasis on Confucianism", New Haven, Ph.D.Diss. Yale University, 1984.

Fu Pei-jung 傅佩榮, *Rudao tianlun fawei* 儒道天論發微 [The Development and Decline of the Confucian and Taoist Theory on Heaven], Taibei (Xuesheng shuju), 1985.

Fu, Pei-jung, "The Confucian Heaven and the Christian God", in Peter K.H. Lee (ed.), *Confucian-Christian Encounters in Historical and Contemporary Perspective*, Lewiston (The Edwin Mellen Press), 1992, 213-222.

Fu Pei-jung 傅佩榮, "Wei *Rudao tianlun fawei* chengqing jidian yiyi" 爲 《儒道天論發微》 澄清幾點疑義 [Clarification of Some Doubtful Points in *The Development and Decline of the Confucian and Taoist Theory on Heaven*], in *Rujia zhexue xinlun* 儒家哲學新論 [New Discussion of Confucian Philosophy], Taibei, 1993, pp. 298-317.

Gilson, Etienne, *The Christian Philosophy of St.Thomas Aquinas*, New York (Random House), 1956.

Gonzáles, J.M., "Semblanzas Mísioneras: P. Francisco Varó, O.P.", *Missionalia Hispanica* 12 (1955), pp.145-191

Gonzáles, J.M., *Historia de las Misiones Dominicanas de China, Vol.V: Bibliógrafias*, Madrid, 1967.

Granet, Marcel, *The Religion of the Chinese People*, (trans. M.Freedman), Oxford (Basil Blackwell), 1975.

Gu Hansong 谷 寒 松 (L. Gutheinz) & Zhao Songqiao 趙 松 喬, *Tianzhulun - Shangdilun: Tiandirenheyi* 天 主 論 · 上 帝 論 ： 天 地 人 合 一 (The Mystery of God: Heaven-Earth-Man: God), Taibei (Guangqi), 1990.

Hall, David L. & Roger T. Ames, *Thinking Through Confucius*, New York (SUNY), 1987.

Henderson, John B., *Scripture, Canon and Commentary: A Comparison of Confucian and Western Exegesis*, Princeton (Princeton University Press), 1991.

Hou Wailu 侯 外 廬 (ed.), *Zhongguo sixiang tongshi (disijuan xia)* 中 國 思 想 通 史 (第 四 卷 下) [Comprehensive History of Chinese Philosophy (IVb)], Beijing, (repr.) 1980.

Huang Yilong 黃 一 農, "'Liyizhizheng' xiangguan wenxian lunshu" 「 禮 儀 之 爭 」 相 關 文 獻 論 述 [Discussion of Documents Related to the Rites Controversy], Draft Version (March 1993), (with permission of the author).

Hucker, Charles O., *A Dictionary of Official Titles in Imperial China*, Taipei (SMC), 1985.

Jiang Hao 江 顥 & Qian Zongwu 錢 宗 武 (transl), *Jinguwen shangshu quanyi* 今 古 文 尚 書 全 譯 [Complete translation of the *Book of Documents*], Guiyang (Guizhou renmin chubanshe), 1990.

Jiang Shanguo 蔣 善 國, *Shangshu zongshu* 尚 書 綜 述 [Summary of the *Book of Documents*], Shanghai, (Guji chubanshe), 1988.

Kalgren, B., "The Book of Documents", *The Museum of Far Eastern Antiquities Bulletin* 22 (1950), pp.1-81.

Kalgren, B., *The Book of Odes*, Stockholm (The Museum of Far Eastern Antiquities), 1950.

Keightley, David N., "The Religious Commitment: Shang Theology and the Genesis of Chinese Political Culture", *History of Religion* 17.3-4 (1978), pp.211-225.

Legge, J., *The Chinese Classics*, Hong Kong, 1885, (repr. Taibei, SMC Publishing Inc.), 1991.

Legge, J., *The Texts of Confucianism: Part I: The Shu King, The Religious Portions of the Shih King, The Hsiâo King*, in F. Max Mühler, *The Sacred Books of the East, Volume III*, Oxford (Clarendon Press), 1879.

Lin Jinshui 林金水, *Mingqingzhiji shidafu yu zhongxi liyizhizheng* 明清之際士大夫與中西禮儀之爭 (Chinese Rites vs. Western Rites: Debates among Traditional Scholars of the Ming-Qing Transitional Period), *Lishi yanjiu* 歷史研究 (1993/2), pp.20-35.

Liu Qiyu 劉起釪, *Shangshu xueshi* 尚書學史 [History of the Study of the *Book of Documents*], Beijing (Zhonghua shuju), 1989.

Lo Kuang 羅光, "Zhongguo dui di--tian de xinyang" 中國對帝－天的信仰 (The Faith in God-Heaven in China), *Collectanea Theologica Universitatis Fujen* 31 (1977), pp.77-103.

Loewe, M., *Early Chinese Texts: A Bibliographical Guide*, Berkeley (Univ. of California), 1993.

Longxi xianzhi 龍溪縣志 [Gazetteer of Longxi District], (1762 (Qianlong 27), 1879 (Guangxu)), (*Zhongguo fangzhi congshu* 中國方志叢書 90).

Major, John S., "Shang-ti", in Mircea Eliade (ed.), *The Encyclopedia of Religion*, London, 1987, vol.XIII, pp.223-224.

Noll, Ray R., (ed.), *100 Roman Documents Concerning the Chinese Rites Controversy (1645-1941)*, Donald F. St. Sure (transl.), San Francisco (Ricci Institute), 1992.

Otto, Rudolf, *The Idea of the Holy*, (transl.J.Harvey), Middlesex (Penguin Books), 1959.

Pelliot, P., *Inventaire sommaire des maunscrits et imprimés chinois de la Bibliothèque Vaticane* (typescript), 13 juin - 6 juillet 1922.

Qu Wanli 屈萬里 (transl.), *Shangshu jinzhu jinyi* 尚書今註今譯 [Annotation and Translation of the Book of Documents], Taibei (Commercial Press), 1984.

Quétif J. & J. Echard, *Scriptores Ordinis Praedicatorum*, Paris, 1721.

Rahner, Karl, "Theos in the New Testament", in *Theological Investigations vol I*, London (Darton, Longman), 1961, pp.79-148.

Rahner, Karl, "The Experience of God Today", in *Theological Investigations vol XI*, London (Darton, Longman), 1974, pp.149-165.

Rahner, Karl, *Foundations of Christian Faith*, (transl.) W. Dych, New York (Crossroad Book), 1978.

Ren Jiyu 任繼愈, *Zhongguo zhexue fazhan shi: xianqin* 中國哲學發展史：先秦 [History of the Development of Chinese Philosophy: Before Qin Dynasty], Beijing (Peoples Publishing House), 1984.

Schoonenberg, P., *De Geest, het Woord en de Zoon*, Averbode (Altiora), 1991.

Shiji 史記 (*Records of the Grand Historian*), Beijing (Zhonghua), Taibei (Minglun), 1972.

Shi(jing) jizhuan 詩〔經〕集傳 [*Book of Odes*], annot. by Zhu Xi 朱熹, (preface 1177), Shanghai (Guji chubanshe), 1991.

Shih, Joseph, "The Notions of God in Ancient Chinese Religion", *Numen* XVI,2 (1969), pp.99-138.

Sinica Franciscana, vol. III, Quarachi, 1936; vol. V, Roma, 1954; vol. VII, Roma, 1965.

Shu(jing) jizhuan 書〔經〕集傳 [*Book of Documents*], annot. by Cai Chen 蔡沈, (preface 1209), Shanghai (Guji chubanshe), 1991.

Shun, Kwong-loi, "Bookreview of Robert Eno, *The Confucian Creation of Heaven*", *Harvard Journal of Asiatic Studies* 52,2 (1992), pp.739-756.

Sishu jizhu 四書集注 [*Four Books*], ed. by Zhu Xi 朱熹 (preface 1177), Taibei (Shijie), 1952.

Streit, R., *Bibiotheca Missionum*, vol. V, Aachen, 1929; vol. VII, Aachen, 1931.

Thompson, Laurence G., "T'ien", in Mircea Eliade (ed.), *The Encyclopedia of Religion*, London, 1987, vol.XIV, pp.508-510.

Tianzhu shiyi 天主實義 (The Solid Meaning of the Lord of Heaven), by Matteo Ricci 利瑪竇, in Wu Xiangxiang 吳相湘 (ed.), *Zhongguo shixue congshu* 中國史學叢書 [Collection on Chinese History], no.23: *Tianxue chuhan* 天學初函 [First Encyclopedia of Heavenly Studies], vol.1, Taibei, (repr.), 1965;

English translation by D. Lancashire and P. Hu Kuo-chen, Taipei/ Paris (Ricci Institute), 1985.

Tien Tchéu-Kang, *L'idée de Dieu dans les huit premiers classiques chinois: Ses noms, son existence et sa nature étudiée à la lumière des découvertes archéologiques*, Fribourg (L'oeuvre St.Justin), 1942.

Van Zoeren, S., *Poetry and Personality: Reading, Exegesis, and Hermeneutics in Traditional China*, Stanford (Stanford Univ. Press), 1991.

von Collani, Claudia, "Charles Maigrot's Role in the Chinese Rites Controversy", unpublished paper Symposium on the Chinese Rites Controversy, San Francisco, Oct. 1992, to be published in D.E. Mungello, (ed.), *The Chinese Rites Controversy: Its History and Meaning*, Sankt Augustin (Steyler), 1995.

Watson, Burton, *Records of the Grand Historian of China*, New York (Columbia Univ.), 1961, 2 vols.

Werner, E.T.C., *A Dictionary of Chinese Mythology*, New York (Julian Press), 1961.

Wu Yu 吳 璵 (transl.), *Xinyi shangshu duben* 新 譯 尚 書 讀 本 [New Translation of the Book of Documents], Taibei (Sanmin shuju), 1989.

Xu Zongze 徐 宗 澤, *MingQingjian yesuhuishi yizhu tiyao* 明 清 間 耶 穌 會 士 譯 著 提 要 [Summary of the Works Translated by the Jesuits in Late Ming and Early Qing], Taibei, 1957.

Yan Mo 嚴 謨: see list of writings in the first chapter of this dissertation.

Ye Xianggao 葉 向 高, "Xixue shijie chujie" 西 學 十 誡 初 解 [First Explanation of the Ten Commandments of Western Learning], in *Cangxia yucao* 蒼 霞 餘 草 [Sequel to the Collected Writings of Ye Xianggao], j.5, p.23a.

Zhou Changyao 周 長 耀, *Jingtian tanyuan* 敬 天 探 源 [Investigation into the Origins of the Veneration of Heaven], Taibei (Shiji shuju), 1981.

Zürcher, Erik, "Jesuit Accommodation and the Chinese Cultural Imperative", unpublished paper Symposium on the Chinese Rites Controversy, San Francisco, Oct. 1992, to be published in D.E. Mungello, (ed.), *The Chinese Rites Controversy: Its History and Meaning*, Sankt Augustin (Steyler), 1995.

Riproduzione anastatica: 5 maggio 1995
Tipografia Poliglotta della Pontificia Università Gregoriana
Piazza della Pilotta, 4 – 00187 Roma